# BASIC GARDENING

A late summer garden featuring beds of various varieties of chrysanthemums. With patience even the beginner can achieve results as glorious as this.

# Basic Gardening

C. E. Pearson

WARD LOCK LIMITED · LONDON

Ward Lock Limited, 116 Baker Street,
London W1M 2BB

*Printed in Great Britain*
*by Richard Clay (The Chaucer Press), Ltd.,*
*Bungay, Suffolk*

# CONTENTS

# 1. THE GARDEN

For many centuries the gardens of Britain have been renowned throughout the world, and of them all, from the formal miniatures of a few square yards to those of several acres, the most famous is the Cottage Garden, a mixture of freedom and formality with flowers growing happily how and where they will, often along the sides of a straight brick path or among the set rows of vegetables.

Except in a very few districts it is not difficult to make and keep a colourful garden. The natural conditions of the country allow a far wider range of trees, shrubs and plants to be grown than is possible under more extreme climates, and by keeping to the commoner and usually more robust varieties the beginner can quickly gain success without undue work or expense, provided the first simple principles of gardening are observed.

The most important thing is thoroughness. Even the simplest job must be done properly, patiently and at the right time. Mistakes can rarely be put right immediately, because by the time they are discovered it is generally too late in the season to have a second try. All the work must therefore be planned methodically, and care be taken to avoid attempting too much at a time. It is always better to grow a few plants well than to have a lot of second-raters. Ambitious programmes and the growing of the more difficult plants should be left until experience and knowledge have been gained.

## TOOLS AND EQUIPMENT

Whether the garden is already established or has yet to be made from a bare plot of land, the first thing to be done is to buy tools. The best qualities and the stainless makes are the cheapest in the long run, being stronger, lighter and easier to use then inferior ones, and if well cared for will last a lifetime.

7

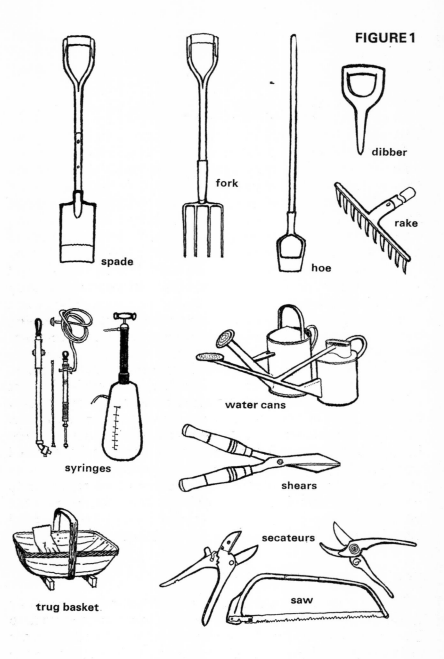

FIGURE 1

spade

fork

hoe

dibber

rake

syringes

water cans

shears

trug basket

secateurs

saw

Many different kinds are available; for the average-sized garden the following will be required:

*Spade* Medium size. No. 2 or 3. Blade almost flat hollowing gently towards the top with shoulders.

*Fork* Four-pronged Digging fork.

*Hoes* Dutch or push hoe for weeding and a Draw hoe, preferably swan-necked, for weeding, drawing drills for seeds and for earthing up.

*Rakes* One heavy, one light, or a medium size 15–18 in. wide, teeth 2 in. deep, $1\frac{1}{2}$ in. apart.

*Line* 30 ft. or more of stout cord on two steel pins 12–18 in. long.

*Measuring sticks* (1) Made from 1-in. batten, 3–6 ft. long with notches cut and picked out in white paint at 6 in., 9 in., 1 ft., 18 in., 2 ft. and 3 ft.

*Wheelbarrow* with wide rubber tyre, of galvanized metal, strong plastic or wood.

*Mowing machine* Power or hand according to the area. Hand machines should be roller-driven, wheeled types being suitable for small areas only.

*Shears* Short-handled type for hedge trimming, long-handled type for lawn edges.

*Edging iron* Half-moon-shaped tool for cutting turf or trimming sides of lawn

*Spraying and dusting equipment* Unless the area is large or has big tall fruit trees, a syringe and small pressure-type of sprayer and a small hand puffer will suffice.

*Roller* with cylinder in two sections. Not heavy.

*Water can* with long spout and detachable rose, of 1- and 2-gal. capacity.

*Sieves* One of $\frac{1}{4}$ in. and one of $\frac{3}{4}$ in. mesh for sifting soil and compost.

*Sundries* Hand trowel and fork, secateurs, hose, pots, seed-boxes, labels, broom, besom, canes, etc.

For tall trees: long-arm pruner and pruning saw.

For constructional work: shovel, rammer, level, straight-edge, builder's trowel and possibly a pick-axe, heavy mattock and crowbar.

For over-grown or rough grass, hedge bottoms or banks:

9

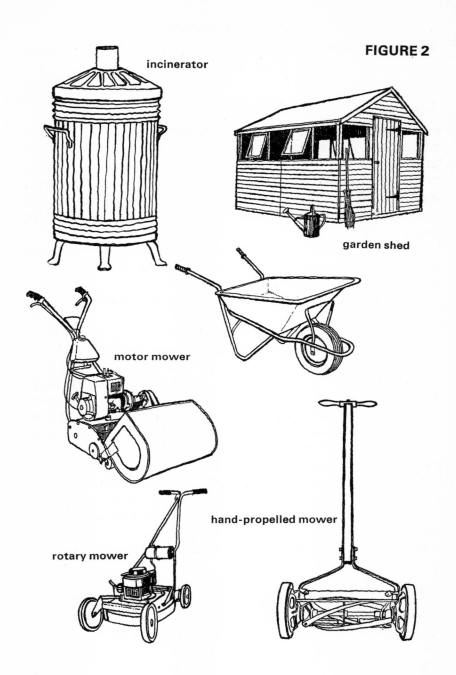

**FIGURE 2**

incinerator

garden shed

motor mower

rotary mower

hand-propelled mower

a sickle or scythe or if the area is appreciable, a rotary mower.

## CARE AND MAINTENANCE

All tools and equipment must be stored under cover, preferably in a well-built, dry, frost-proof shed which can be used also for storing fertilizers, bulbs, fruit and vegetables. The floor space should be reserved for the barrow and mowing machine, the walls should have strong hooks for the larger tools and shelves for the smaller ones, and the roof may have battens nailed across to carry canes and stakes.

After use, all tools should be cleaned, dried and wiped with an oily rag. A wedge-shaped piece of wood or a decorator's scraper for scraping off soil, and a spoke-brush for cleaning the blades and parts of a mowing machine are necessary.

Every tool must be used properly and for its particular purpose. Spades and forks can be ruined if used as levers, and cutting tools, such as shears and secateurs, can easily be damaged if forced to do a bigger job than they are made for.

The gardener should train himself to work steadily and unhurriedly and get to know how much he can do in a given time and what is the most comfortable way of working. Many may find left-handed working is better and some may be able to change easily from right to left. Kneeling on a pad is far less tiring than stooping when hand-weeding or singling.

It is a good plan to start off with the heavy jobs and do the lighter ones later in the day, and many unnecessary journeys will be saved if all the tools likely to be used are taken out in the barrow at the start, and a sharp knife or secateurs and some string and raffia are always kept in the pocket.

# 2. SOIL AND SITE

Soil is generally a complex mixture of inorganic or mineral matter formed by the age-old erosion of rocks, and organic matter of vegetable or animal origin loosely called humus. Microscopic organisms such as bacteria live in the soil and play an important part in forming plant-food. According to its composition, soil varies from good to bad. Fortunately much can be done to improve the bad, and often the improvement comes quickly.

There are six main types, grouped according to the character of the surface soil or the top 9 in. Below this is the sub-soil, which may be of very different character.

## TYPES OF SOIL

*Sandy soils* Light and easy to work, generally deficient in plant-food and humus; often dry out quickly, especially where the proportion of sand is high.

*Clay soils* Heavy, sticky, difficult to work, generally deficient in humus; hold moisture well, but usually cake or crack in dry weather; often need draining.

*Chalk soils* Usually shallow and deficient in humus; sticky and difficult to work if the amount of chalk is high, but good "marl" soils if it is low.

*Gravel soils* Poor, dry, hungry soils; difficult and costly to improve.

*Peaty soils* Warm, easy to work; generally fertile, but may be sour and acid, lacking lime.

*Loams* Mixtures of various kinds; generally fertile, fairly easy to work and capable of growing a wide range of crops. According to their composition are known as sandy loams, clay loams or peaty loams.

*Sub-soil* is usually different from the surface soil in both texture and composition. A light sandy soil lying on a heavy sub-soil may benefit from the water held below but a gravelly sub-soil usually robs the surface of moisture and makes growing difficult. Sometimes a hard layer or pan occurs between two soils, due to natural formation or to constant cultivation at a fixed depth. Double-digging will be necessary to break it up (see p. 15).

## SOIL TEXTURE

Physical condition or texture is as important as fertility. It usually depends on the amount of humus present and the methods of cultivation. Good texture provides the best conditions for root growth; it encourages soil organisms, allows air and warmth to penetrate and prevents water-logging, yet helps to retain moisture in dry seasons.

## DRAINAGE

The lighter soils and those on slopes or overlying a porous sub-soil usually drain naturally. Those that are heavy and often sodden or squelchy in winter or show weeds such as sedges, rushes, horse-tail or marsh buttercup, need some form of artificial drainage to make them suitable for gardening. But drainage is a big job, and as it is possible to "over-drain", care must be exercised before the work is started. A few holes 2–3 ft. deep should be dug out and the soil-section examined. If after a day or two they do not hold water but the surrounding soil is wet, the trouble may be due to a pan or inefficient cultivation. If they hold water, draining will be necessary.

*Planning* Drains should be laid not less than $2\frac{1}{2}$ ft. and not more than 4 ft. deep and each line or lateral should be 15 ft. to 20 ft. apart with a fall of not less than 1 in 100. If the area to be drained is small or a narrow strip, one line may be sufficient, but if two or more lines are required or the garden slopes towards the centre, a main drain into which the laterals can empty will be necessary. Laterals should always enter the main obliquely, in the direction of the fall and not at right angles. The outlet should be into a ditch if possible, but in most gardens it has to be into a soakaway made at the lowest point, in a corner or under a path.

A scale plan should be drawn and the lines of the drains marked carefully. The trenches should then be excavated in the form of a V and kept as narrow as possible in order to lessen the work, the top-soil being thrown up on one side and the sub-soil on the other so that they can be returned in the proper order. The bottom of the trench is finished off by using a spirit-level and straight-edge resting on short pegs. A first peg is driven in to the level required and a second one at the other end of the straight-edge made level with it. This is then tapped in further to give the necessary fall and becomes in its turn the first peg for the next length, and so on down the trench.

*Types of drain* Although expensive, pipe drains are best and last longest. The most suitable are plain porous pipes, 2–3 in. in diameter, laid end to end without any cement at the joints, except where a lateral enters a main or the main empties into a ditch or soakaway, where it should be built round with brick or stone and cemented. Cheaper methods are to fill the bottom of the trench with a 4–6 in. layer of broken brick or hard clinker or to lay bundles of brushwood made up of branches about 1 to $1\frac{1}{2}$ in. in diameter. Such drains work well and last for many years especially if they are first covered with turves before filling in the trench.

Whatever type of drain is used the soil should be put back gently to begin with, the rest being shovelled in and allowed to settle naturally.

*Soakaways* A soakaway should not be less than 4 ft. by 4 ft. and 4 ft. deep. The top-soil and sub-soil should be taken out and stacked separately and the rest excavated and wheeled away. The hole is then filled to within 18 in. of the top with rubble, brick or hard clinker and the soil put back.

## CLEARING A NEW SITE

All bricks, stones and rubbish should be collected and stacked in a heap; they may be useful later on. Brambles and self-sown thorns should be grubbed up and burnt, but no tree or shrub

**'Gold Cup',
a floribunda rose.**

**'Polka', a floribunda rose with an old world fragrance.**

**Standard roses such as the variety shown above
are excellent for growing in beds or grass.**

should be removed until the final plan for the garden has been made. Long matted grass should be cut off and stacked for compost (p. 35). For this the best tool is a scythe, but surprising progress can be made with a sickle or shears if the work is done steadily and methodically. The turf will then be more easily dug in, but some may be fit to leave for a lawn. On good soil mowing, rolling, weeding and feeding will often turn old or neglected pasture into good quality turf in a surprisingly short time.

## DIGGING

Digging is the most important of all garden work because it has such a great effect on soil texture. It must therefore be done properly. There are two forms, single-digging where the soil is moved to one spade's depth (9 in.) and double-digging, sometimes called bastard trenching, where the soil is moved to two spades' depth. Except where the top-soil is very thin and the sub-soil unsuitable, the spade should always be inserted to its full depth and as nearly upright as possible and the soil lifted and turned right over. But there is nothing to be gained in trying to lift the biggest slice possible; a convenient spadeful should be the aim and the way to control its size and weight, particularly on the heavier soils, is to make a cut along the side of the slice at right angles to its face. The work must be kept level and each row of digging turned into the trench left by the previous row. If there is any difficulty in forming a trench to begin with the best way is to dig out the first row and barrow it away to where the digging will finish, when it will be ready for filling up the last trench of all.

In double-digging, a trench *must* be made at the beginning. It should be 10 in. deep, and at least 15 in. or preferably up to 20 in. wide. If the plot can be divided into two strips so that the work proceeds down one half and back up the other, the digging will end alongside where it begins and barrowing will be reduced to the minimum. After the first trench is opened, the sub-soil is dug over with a fork, manure or compost added and the top-soil of the next trench put on top. This leaves the next row of sub-soil ready for forking and so on down the plot. It is hard slow work, but is well worth the effort when dealing with new sites, any turf present being pared off as the digging proceeds, chopped up and forked in with the sub-soil.

**FIGURE 3** This simple diagram shows the lines along which a spade should be inserted.

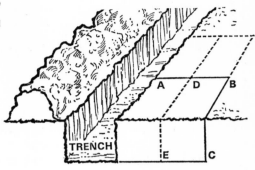

An attractive bed of Californian poppies. These
are hardy annuals for sowing in April and May.

A border of elegantly spraying Coral Bells (Heuchera).

A delightful border of delicate 'Coral Satin' petunias.

# 3. LAYOUT AND PLANNING

The art of planning a new garden or remaking an old one lies in making the best use of a particular site. Model plans cannot always be followed because the size of the garden, its aspect, shape, surroundings and levels will generally vary, and what appeals to one gardener may have little interest for another.

Scale plans are essential. Measure the outside boundaries, the position of the house, drive or main path, and plot them on paper to a scale of not less than 1 in. to 10 ft. Two foolscap sheets will usually be sufficient for a small garden, one for the front, one for the back. Mark north, south, east and west and any adjoining features such as a high building or tall trees that cast heavy shade. Note on different days and at different times how the sun strikes or if cutting winds run down one side of the house. See what kind of gardens look best in the locality and make a list of the trees, shrubs and plants that seem to flourish happily in the district.

In most cases, unless there is ample space, the front garden with its drive and entrance must be of formal design consisting of lawn or paving, with shrubs, roses and one or two formal beds. The design of the back garden should be more natural as far as shape and size allow.

## HOUSE AND GARDEN

Gardens should always be designed so that the best parts can be seen from the principal rooms of the house. The main features should be ones that hold interest for a comparatively long time, such as herbaceous borders, roses or flowering shrubs, with a bed for planting out to give colour from spring to autumn.

The most common problem is how to treat the long narrow garden or one that tapers to a point. The best way is to break the appearance of length by introducing some feature that makes the nearest part of the plot roughly square. Such a division should not run the whole way across but have a wide opening in the centre or be in two parts, one coming from each side with at least 10 ft. between their lines. It should, too, be something that can be seen through, such as a pergola or row of cordons, so that the rest of the garden is visible and any feeling of being shut in is avoided.

Whatever the size or shape of a garden, certain general principles should be observed. They will save much work and expense.

*General* Don't try to get too much into a given space. Give each feature plenty of room and the gardener room to work. The tool-shed, compost heap and bonfire space form the workshop of the garden; elbow room is essential. They must be served by a good path connecting up with all parts of the garden.

*Paths* As few as necessary and wide enough, at least 3 ft., to take the barrow or mower. Avoid narrow, serpentine designs.

A path leading out of sight behind bushes or shrubs makes an interesting feature.

*Steps* Not less than 3 ft. wide except in a rock-garden or if part of a formal design, such as a rose or herb garden. They should never be in a main path that has to carry the barrow or mower.

*Trees and shrubs* Find out how big they will grow and allow space accordingly, especially if planted near the house, drive or a path.

*Formal beds* Bedding out means work and expense. One or two large beds look better than several little ones.

*Lawns* Avoid narrow points or angles; they are difficult to mow and prevent the easy turning of the machine. Anything set into a lawn, e.g. a bed, means more edge-trimming. Clumps of bulbs interrupt mowing and must be left until the foliage has died down. If wanted they should be planted in a crescent shape so that the mower can run close to them. Stepping-stones must be set firmly at the right level, just below the surface of the turf so that the mower passes over safely but does not leave a lot of grass to be cut by hand. Where a new house is built in a grass field, a good lawn can often be made from the original turf and, unless wanted for games, levelling is unnecessary and usually undesirable.

*Artificial edgings* Tiles, stones, wood, etc., often get out of line and are difficult to weed. Grass borders look good if well kept, but they have two edges to trim and if too narrow are difficult to mow and often break down. They should be at least 3 ft. wide.

*Levelling, excavation, filling up* Plan some feature nearby to take or give the soil so as to reduce the amount of barrowing.

*Tall trees and ornamentals* must be carefully sited since few flowers or vegetables will grow well underneath. Fruit trees are generally not suited to a small garden; birds take the buds and spraying is difficult or impossible if other plants are grown underneath.

*Plants for fences and walls* must be chosen carefully so as not to interfere with painting or repairs. For wooden fences climbing roses, blackberries or loganberries are suitable. For the walls of the house the more pliable climbers such as rose, jasmine, honeysuckle, etc., should be chosen because they can be lowered away when painting has to be done, especially if grown on a trellis which should be hooked, not nailed to the wall. Creepers and ivy should not be used. Warm, sunny walls of brick may be reserved for peaches or pears; in this position a hanging net can be used as protection against birds.

*Natural features* Sloping ground lends itself to walls, terraces or banks. If it slopes away from the house, the walls or terraces should be planned as bold semi-circular features more or less at right angles to the house and not parallel with it, otherwise it will be only the neighbours who enjoy the garden.

## MARKING OUT

With these general principles in mind, the main features decided upon should be pencilled into the outline plan and provisionally marked out in the garden. Key points should be marked with strong canes, 3 ft. or 4 ft. long, and intermediate points with shorter canes. For the lines of paths, walls or steps, stakes 2 ft. long and stout enough to be hammered in should be used, because many of them will outline constructional work which may not be started for some time.

Imagination will help to picture how the results will look from different viewpoints and suggest alterations. The final plan should be drawn accurately and all canes and stakes adjusted and set firm. If, as the work proceeds, any further alteration suggests itself a new provisional plan should be drawn, because so often one change will affect other parts of the original scheme and they in turn may have to be replanned.

For measuring long distances, a 33-ft. or 66-ft. tape is best, but a line of strong cord with the 10-ft. intervals marked with paint can be used. If the cord is not tarred, it must be kept dry,

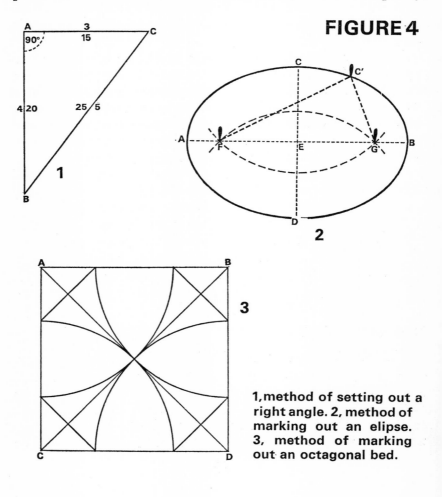

# FIGURE 4

1, method of setting out a right angle. 2, method of marking out an elipse. 3, method of marking out an octagonal bed.

since it will shorten considerably when wet. Two measuring sticks, straight-edges and a level will also be needed.

*Measuring right angles* For most kinds of garden construction a right-angled frame is essential. It can be made by joining three strong battens measuring 3 ft., 4 ft. and 5 ft. respectively or half these lengths if a smaller triangle is required. The battens must be cut accurately and secured at each corner with at least two screws.

*Marking curves or circles* A stout stake should be driven in to mark the centre and a line with a loop at the end slipped over. Another loop is then made at the distance required to take another stake or steel pin which can be used to mark out the curve or circle required.

To mark out an oval bed two lines equal to the maximum length and breadth desired should be set out so as to divide each other equally and at right angles. AB, CD, Fig. 4. With a radius equal to half the length of AB mark two arcs from points C and D and drive in two stakes where they intersect at F and G. Then take a cord or line with a loop at each end and equal in length to AB. Slip the loops over the stakes F and G and with a sharp stick $C^1$, placed inside the looped cord, trace the outline of the oval, keeping the cord tight.

## LEVELLING

Any big job of levelling means a lot of hard work and must be planned carefully beforehand in order to reduce the labour as much as possible. The surface soil should be stripped off and stacked to one side and the desired level set and marked with a row of stout, straight-topped pegs. As the work of excavation or filling up proceeds, more pegs should be driven in, all carefully set to the same level by using a straight-edge and spirit-level. Planks should be laid down for wheeling the barrow and if moved frequently will help to consolidate the made-up soil. The sub-soil of any excavated portion should be forked over, and the whole area levelled roughly. The top-soil should then be put back and raked level, using the garden line stretched taut from peg to peg as a guide, and rolled. Several weeks should be allowed for natural settling before the final raking and levelling is done.

# 4. CONSTRUCTION AND MAINTENANCE

A sound boundary fence, not less than 4 ft. high, proof against dogs and in some areas cattle and rabbits, is essential. Even where hedges are to be planted alongside, the protecting fence must be well constructed, strong enough for its job and good enough to last for many years. Wooden posts, preferably oak, should be coated with preservative and iron posts painted. They should be set 10–12 ft. apart, sunk into the ground at least 2 ft. deep and rammed firm or concreted. Where wire netting is used it should be of 2–3-in. mesh, or, if rabbits are about, of 1-in. mesh, and should then be sunk into the ground 6 in. deep, with the edge turning outwards to prevent burrowing.

*Post and wire* fencing consists of heavy gauge galvanized wires about 1 ft. apart, stretched taut and stapled to posts. Wire netting is generally added. The posts should be not less than 2 in. × 2 in., and have straining posts for support at every 60–100 ft. and at the corners.

*Chestnut pale* fencing made of cleft pales bound in galvanized wire can be bought in various heights ready for setting up on posts.

*Chain link* fencing of various mesh and designs is also available. It makes a sound and durable boundary.

*Close-boarded* fencing may be of oak, fir, larch or other wood. Cleft oak is the most lasting. The main posts should be 4–5 in. square, connected with cant rails to which the boards are nailed. Gravel boards at least 6 in. × 1 in. should be provided at the base.

*Wattle hurdles* set up on post and wire are particularly useful in exposed situations where immediate protection is wanted. They last for several years, but look unsightly when deterioration begins.

**FIGURE 5**

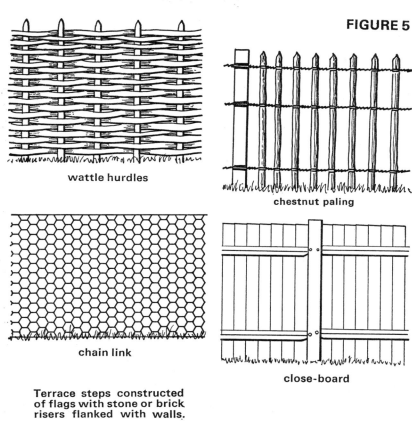

wattle hurdles

chestnut paling

chain link

close-board

Terrace steps constructed of flags with stone or brick risers flanked with walls.

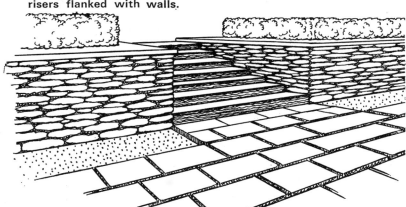

## HEDGES

Great care should be taken when planting a new hedge; mistakes cannot be put right afterwards. The soil should be deeply dug 3 ft. wide and manure or compost forked in. The plants should be young, not above 2–3 ft. high, and be set 1–2 ft. apart according to the species, which must be able to withstand cutting to the height desired, grow well, but not so well that it gets out of hand, and not have a wide root-spread that will interfere with other crops. A protecting fence will generally be necessary for the first five or six years.

*Evergreens* In spite of its common use, there is still much to be said for privet particularly the golden variety which is the less vigorous. Privet grows well on nearly all soils and if it gets out of hand will stand drastic cutting back. The evergreen honeysuckle (*Lonicera*) is also generally suitable, but must be hard-clipped in its early years if bare patches at the base are to be avoided. Cypresses of various kinds are not always successful. They require careful cutting and often, after a severe winter, die back in patches. Yew, holly and evergreen oak make good hedges but are slow to grow in the early years.

*Deciduous* The common thorn and cherry plum grow well almost everywhere and will stand hard cutting. Beech is especially useful on chalky soils, and hornbeam on heavy clays.

*Ornamental* Many flowering shrubs may be used, but they form no boundary against cattle or sheep unless a sound protecting fence is also maintained. Flowering currant, escallonia, and various species of viburnum and berberis, particularly *B. stenophylla* and *B. darwinii* are the most generally suitable.

*Care and Maintenance* Hedges should be clipped to a point to allow air and light to penetrate and prevent snow lodging on the top and breaking the branches. Clipping should generally be done twice a year, in May and again in August or September, the flowering hedges being trimmed after flowering. For large-leaved plants such as laurel, secateurs should be used instead of shears which cut through the leaves and cause them to wither and look unsightly. Hedges which have got out of hand should be cut back in March.

# PATHS

Main paths which have to carry heavy loads should be not less than 3 ft. wide, straight or only slightly curved, well-built, flat and, where possible, laid level with the adjoining soil. Convex surfaces are necessary only for very wide paths. Brick, stone, crazy paving or gravel look best; concrete, asphalt and tarmac should be restricted to the kitchen garden.

*Foundations* The line of the path should be marked out with stout pegs 2 ft. long and soil excavated to a depth of 6 in. or so according to the kind of path and the load it will have to carry. The foundation should be a layer of rubble or clinker, followed by 1–2 in. of ashes, both rammed firmly.

*Gravel, asphalt or tarmac* A layer 2 in. thick is laid on the foundation and rolled. There must be a firm edge to the sides of the path, such as a wall, strip of concrete or a row of bricks or stone laid in cement.

*Concrete* Boards 1 in. thick and 6–9 in. wide must first be laid along the sides of the path and secured with pegs on the outside. Concrete 2–3 in. thick is worked down, roughly smoothed, allowed to set and finished off with a top layer of cement.

*Stone flags* 1–2 in. of sand should be put on top of the ashes and the stones firmly bedded in, breaking the joints. The spaces may be filled with cement mortar brought up to just below the level of the flags. The stones should be $1\frac{1}{2}$–$2\frac{1}{2}$ in. thick and not less than the equivalent of one foot square.

*Crazy paving* The stones should be laid in sand with or without cement, with the space between not more than an average of 1 in. wide. The minimum size should be the same as for flags, since small stones easily get displaced.

*Bricks* should generally be laid in mortar, bonded or keyed to a pattern. A half-brick may be left out here and there to leave space for a plant.

# CONCRETE AND CEMENT MIX

| CONCRETE | CEMENT |
|---|---|
| 4 parts gravel | 3 parts sand |
| 2   „   sand | 1   „   cement |
| 1   „   cement | |

# PAVING

Walks and terraces may be paved with stone or brick or a combination of both, and various patterns and designs can be worked out. If laid in sand, the corners or outside rows should be cemented to keep the whole area firm. On a broad terrace, stone flags should be laid in line longitudinally, the joints being broken laterally.

## BEDS AND BORDERS

After marking out, the soil should be double-dug, manure or compost forked in, and time allowed for settling when the surface should be raked over so that it rises slightly from the edges of the bed.

Herbaceous borders should be planned carefully before any plants are set out and should generally have a background such as an evergreen hedge, shrubbery or pergola.

## LAWNS

A well-kept lawn is attractive all the year round. After the initial expenditure, the annual cost is small; regular and careful attention is the important thing.

New lawns are made by turfing or sowing seed, and the most suitable soils are the light or medium loams. A heavy soil should first be improved with sand, and a light soil with short, well-decayed manure. The work should begin in the early autumn, the soil being limed and drained if necessary, levelled and allowed to settle. After settling, further raking and levelling will generally be necessary, removing any young weeds and stones, and adding bone meal 2 oz. per sq. yd.

*Laying turf* Turves should be of high quality grass, $1\frac{1}{2}$–2 in. thick, 3 ft. long and 1 ft. wide, and laid straight against the garden line, breaking the joints in each row. They must be well firmed down with a turf beater or spade, rolled and if necessary, watered. Fine soil should be brushed into any cracks or small holes, and any hollows must be filled up under the turf.

*Sowing seed* High-quality seed treated with a bird repellent

26

is essential. It should be sown in September or April at 2 or 3 oz. per sq. yd. when the soil is dry enough for easy raking and there is no wind. A few days before sowing, a dressing of lawn fertilizer or sulphate of ammonia should be raked in. Half the seed should be sown evenly across the plot and half at right angles, and raked in lightly both ways. It is a great help if the edges of the area to be sown are made up with turves.

When the grass is 1–2 in. high any weeds and stones should be removed and a light rolling given. A few days later it should be mown with the machine set high.

*Management (early Spring)* Sweep and rake lightly; feed with a proprietary dressing or sulphate of ammonia $\frac{1}{2}$ oz. per sq. yd. or, if the soil is poor, increase to 1 oz. and give also 2 oz. bone meal and $\frac{1}{2}$ oz. sulphate of potash. If many small weeds are present dress with lawn sand or selective weed-killer in May.

*Mowing* During the season cut the edges and mow regularly at least once a week. For the rest of the year, including winter, mow as required (with the machine set higher) except when the soil is very wet.

*Rolling* Use a light roller three or four times a year; never roll when the soil is wet. If a power-driven mower with roller is used, its weight is generally sufficient on most soils and additional rolling is not necessary.

*Worms* If in excess use a worm-killer, otherwise brush casts away regularly.

*Water* when necessary, giving an ample supply.

# PERGOLAS

Pergolas are prominent and permanent features and must therefore appear to have a purpose in the general design. They may serve as a background to a border, a division between two parts of the garden or as a double row over a paved walk from the house to a sitting-out place or a summer house. The uprights may be wooden posts or brick or stone pillars with wooden cross-beams and corner pieces. The construction must be sound enough to withstand the weight of rain and pressure of wind on the climbers when fully grown, but the number of cross-pieces and corner-pieces should be kept to the minimum, otherwise the pergola will look "all wood". The best wood is oak, especially on pillars, but larch and pine are cheaper and easier to work.

The height should be at least 7 ft. and the posts or pillars 10–12 ft. apart. Posts should be sunk 3 ft. deep with that part stripped of its bark and well-coated with preservative. Pillars of brick or stone should be 18 in. square, with the courses bonded and built on a good concrete foundation, 1 ft. thick. Double rows should be 8–10 ft. apart, the main tie-beams 5 in. × 4 in. and the cross-pieces 4 in. × 3 in.

Although rambler and climbing roses are the general favourites, other plants are equally suitable (see p. 57). A mixture of three or four kinds adds greatly to the attraction.

**FIGURE 6**

In a rock garden the stones should be set firmly to lean slightly backwards and downwards at the same angle.

# WALLS

Walls should never stand by themselves but always be a part of the garden design. They look best associated with a terrace or steps and should then be made of the same material, or they may form the face of a bank, when the wall should be of stone and built "dry". Plants to be grown in the wall should be set as the work proceeds, planting firmly at the base of a vertical joint and avoiding any air pockets around the roots.

*Terrace walls* A wall acting as a support to a terrace should slope slightly inwards towards its top. Bricks should be laid in mortar, bonded and built up on a concrete foundation 2–3 in. thick and 1 ft. wide. Stone walls may be built dry unless the stones are no bigger than an ordinary brick. There must be no air pockets in or behind the wall.

Walls built above the level of a terrace should be not less than 18 in. or more than $2\frac{1}{2}$ ft. high, set in mortar, and either built solid and topped with rectangular flags large enough to project 2 in. on both sides, or made with a cavity to form a bed for plants. The bed should be at least 9 in. across, otherwise it will dry out rapidly in summer.

*Dry walls* The stones should be at least 2 in. thick, roughly rectangular, and not less than the equivalent of 6 in. × 6 in. in area. They should be laid sloping slightly backwards on a foundation of rammed soil, bonded as far as possible, with $\frac{1}{2}$–1 in. of good soil between the layers and 1–2 in. between each stone. The largest stones should be put at the bottom with a few at intervals higher up to act as ties. The wall may be topped with flags or soil in which trailing plants may be grown.

# ROCK GARDEN

The main purpose of a rock garden is to enable the gardener to grow certain plants which require particular conditions different from those given by an ordinary bed or border. In their natural environment most rock plants enjoy an open situation, a good supply of moisture, perfect drainage, protection for their roots and, perhaps the most important thing of all, good soil, although many need little of it. Cold winters and hot summers are the ideal, but many rock plants will flourish in Britain as long as dampness and shade are avoided.

Unless these general conditions can be reasonably well imitated, any attempt to build a rock garden will end in disappointment. The site must be of reasonable size, sunny and free from the shade of trees and any risk of waterlogging. It should be on a slope, either natural or artificial. The stones should be of limestone or hard sandstone, the smallest being roughly equal to an area of 2 ft. × 2 ft. They should be set in the soil leaning slightly backwards at a uniform angle, in imitation of a natural outcrop, and carefully bedded in so that no air pockets are left.

Planting should be done in the spring, the plants being set towards the lower end of the sloping rocks, where the roots can find moisture and protection. Artificial watering may be necessary during summer and protection for the more delicate species in winter. Every year a light dressing of peat or old compost should be forked in, and after the plants have flowered the old growths should be trimmed off.

## WATER GARDEN

In a small garden, the formal rectangular or oval pool is generally the most suitable. Anything larger or more elaborate, such as an imitation stream, requires considerable space and should only be attempted where it is obviously suggested by the natural shape of the land. Pools should never be made under or close to trees; the falling leaves decompose and spoil the water, and the roots may damage the base.

Prefabricated pools of various shapes are now available and are perfectly satisfactory for most small gardens. The soil should be excavated to make a good fit, particularly along the bottom in order to avoid any strain on the material. For more informal shapes plastic sheeting may be used, and here again the excavation must be neatly finished off to avoid undue stretching. The edges of the pool may be concealed with rocks or flags which, on a sheeted pool, must be heavy enough to hold the sheets in position.

If a concrete pool is to be built it should not be less than 2 ft. or more than 4 ft. deep, and when excavation is started an extra 6 in. should be allowed all round. After the soil has been dug out, the bottom and sides should be rammed hard and damped before concreting. The concrete should be at least 5–6 in. thick, well worked down and left rough. The bottom is laid first, and after it has set, the side walls are built up by filling in between the soil and well-supported wooden shuttering. When dry, a top layer of 2 in. of cement is put on carefully with a trowel. An inlet pipe and overflow should be arranged and a plug and drainhole may be fixed in the bottom. The sides may be topped with flags, rocks or turf.

In pools of oval or irregular shape the bottom may slope gradually towards one end to form a beach where fish can sun themselves, and another part may have an inner wall to form a marsh garden. This wall should be about 2 in. below the level of the water.

The water plants should be set in baskets filled with soil and lowered to the bottom, or in pockets held in position by rocks. The plants should not be set until a month after the pool has been made and filled with water, and fish should not be put in until 2–3 months later.

## MAINTENANCE

While the key to construction is never to take on more than can be done thoroughly and unhurriedly with the time and facilities that are available, the key to maintenance is to keep level with the work as it comes along. The quickest and least tiring way of doing so is to carry out all the various jobs at the optimum time. But it is not always easy to judge when that time has arrived, and the week-end gardener who has many other calls on his spare time often finds difficulty in fitting the work in conveniently. It is mainly a matter of planning and looking ahead and it is well to remember that disappointment will as often follow when a job is done too soon as when it is left until too late. For example, it is not always easy to pick the best time for sowing. The instruction on a packet of seed may say "Sow in April or May" but if April's weather is cold and wet nothing will be gained by sowing then. Better results will come from sowing in May, waiting until the soil has warmed up and is in a more suitable condition for germination and seedling growth. On the other hand, jobs such as staking and tying or weeding can rarely be done too soon. If put off, they invariably add extra work and trouble; no amount of tying will restore a plant to its normal shape and growth once its stems have been battered or twisted by wind and rain or simply left to fall about as they will, and if weeds are allowed to grow too big they cannot be hoed off and left to die, but instead, they must be carried away, which in itself is an extra and tiresome job. Modern weed-killers will, of course, save a great deal of time and labour but they have certain limits, and to get their full results they, too, must be used at the best times. Weed-killers containing simazin will keep paths free of weeds for the whole season if applied at the end of March or in early April, whereas those containing paraquat and the "selectives" such as are used on lawns, are most successful when their application is deferred until the warmer weather comes in May or June. If mowing is postponed, it not only becomes harder as each day goes by but it also allows the coarser grasses to smother the finer ones, and if autumn clearing is put off many plants will shed seeds which will give rise to undesirable seedlings. Most garden plants are hybrids and hybrids rarely reproduce themselves exactly from seed but instead, give rise to seedlings which often vary widely from one another and from the parent, some of them growing so vigorously that they quickly smother that parent which may be less robust but far more desirable. It is because of these variations that most perennials are multiplied vegetatively instead of from seed.

A good "Garden Calendar" will help a beginner to keep to time but it will inevitably contain far more information than he may want for the simple reason that it must include many kinds of plants that he will not be growing or even wish to grow in his particular garden. The best kind of calendar is one that a gardener makes up for himself to fit his own requirements. It takes a few years of experience to get it complete but it grows quickly and easily out of an ordinary notebook in which all sorts of information about the garden can be recorded. It should contain plans of beds and borders and the names of the plants or shrubs growing in them because labels have a habit

A border of delphiniums. This stately flower is
also excellent for the herbaceous border.

Several varieties of iris. Here they are
used as an edging plant for a brick walk.

A striking display of firethorn (Pyracantha) berries
One of the many advantages of shrubs is
that they are attractive when in flower and fruiting.

A garden in full summer blossom. To create a garden
like this is really worth all the time and effort involved.

of getting lost, and notes should be made of any changes that may be necessary, particularly of any shrub or plant that needs moving to a more suitable position. Dates of sowing, planting or taking cuttings should also be recorded together with the results obtained, particularly the poor ones, because it is often as easy to learn from mistakes and failures as from successes. And if the book records such things as the number of plants or bulbs required to fill a bed or the quantities of fertilizers or weed-killers needed to dress the lawn or other parts of the garden, a great deal of time can be saved since there will be no need to do the calculations as every new season comes round.

# 5. FEEDING THE PLANTS

Plants live by breathing through their leaves and absorbing dissolved food through their roots. Inside the plant the materials are converted into new tissue and growth results. Provided other conditions such as climate and environment are satisfactory, it is the amount of available food in the soil that determines whether a plant grows well or badly. And when it has grown, the gardener often removes the whole or a part; flowers are picked, lawns are mown and fruit and vegetables are gathered. This is equivalent to taking plant food away from the soil and the loss must be made good by adding manure if the level of fertility is to be maintained or increased.

The principal plant foods, known as the essential elements, are compounds of nitrogen, phosphorus, potassium and calcium, the last three being commonly called phosphorus, potash and lime. Others, such as iron, manganese, magnesium, etc., are required in small quantities only. They are known as minor elements, and are generally present in sufficient quantities in a well-managed soil that is regularly and properly manured. Signs of their deficiency are curiously coloured leaves, malformed shoots or premature leaf-fall.

Some plants require more of a certain food than others. The various grasses in a lawn require a good supply of nitrogen, but peas and beans and lupins can do with only small amounts because they are helped by certain bacteria which form nodules on their roots and enable them to make use of the free nitrogen in the air. Knowing what the different groups of plants require, and knowing also that the different plant foods have specific effects on growth, makes it possible to manure correctly and economically.

*Nitrogen* encourages quick growth and a good green colour. It is specially useful for young growing plants once they have become established and for crops grown for their leaves, e.g., cabbages. Excess leads to over-luxuriant growth.

*Potash* is essential for general health and as a balancing safeguard against excess of other foods. It helps in the flowering and ripening stages and in building up resistance to disease.

*Phosphates* also help in the ripening stages, but their main value lies in their power to encourage good root growth.

*Lime* is not only a plant food but also has a most beneficial effect on texture, especially on heavy soils, and counteracts acidity.

## TYPES OF MANURE

There are two main groups, organic manures of animal or vegetable origin and inorganic or artificially made chemical compounds. In both groups there are quick-acting and slow-acting kinds which enable the gardener to give his plants a tonic or a lasting feed.

*Organic manures* Farmyard manure, the most valuable of all, is a complete plant food, helps to increase humus and improve soil texture, and makes an excellent base to which other specific fertilizers can be added. The composition varies according to the feeding of the animals and the bedding they use. Sawdust and wood shavings decrease the value, as they decompose much more slowly than straw.

*Compost* is next best to farmyard manure and has the added advantage that it can be made in the garden. All waste plant material that is not diseased should be saved and put on the compost heap. This should be 4–7 ft. wide, up to 5 ft. high and any length. It should be built up in alternate layers of 9–12 in. of plant material and 2 in. of animal manure. In place of the manure, a sprinkling of sulphate of ammonia or a proprietary "accelerator" may be used, adding chalk or powdered limestone (not quick lime) at every foot in height if sulphate of ammonia is chosen. The heap soon warms up as decomposition begins, then cools down after a few weeks, when it should be turned. Working from one end, the sides should be turned into the centre and the layers well mixed and left for two or three months, when the compost will be dark, short, well broken down and ready for digging in. A brick or concrete lined pit is better than a heap because it warms up more quickly and needs no turning.

*Poultry manure* is rich in nitrogen and also contains phosphates and potash. Unless dry, it cannot be stored satisfactorily and is generally best used as the animal manure in the compost heap.

Various *animal wastes* make excellent manures. Guano, dried blood, meat meal and fish manure are quick-acting and rich in nitrogen; shoddy, hoof and horn and various kinds of bone manures act more slowly but last longer. The bone manures contain high proportions of phosphates.

*Green manuring* is the practice of growing a quick, bulky crop for digging in to add to the humus in the soil. The most suitable is Italian ryegrass sown broadcast at $\frac{1}{2}$ oz. per sq. yd. When ready for digging, sulphate of ammonia $\frac{1}{2}$ oz. per sq. yd. should first be sprinkled on the crop. It is most valuable on dry or hungry soils.

*Inorganic manures* Sulphate of ammonia is generally the most suitable nitrogenous fertilizer, quick-acting and specially useful for top-dressings intended to push a crop on. Other nitrogenous fertilizers are nitrate of lime, calcium cyanamide and nitrate of potash, the last being highly concentrated and best suited for use on glasshouse crops.

The most common phosphatic fertilizer is super-phosphate of lime, which becomes more readily available in the soil than various kinds of rock phosphate. Basic slag is slower in action but more lasting.

The best form of potash is sulphate of potash. Kainit and muriate of potash are cheaper but less concentrated.

The most suitable forms of lime are finely powdered hydrated lime, ground limestone or chalk, and should be spread over the soil after digging. Quick lime should only be used in winter, on heavy or acid soils.

*Compound fertilizers* Mixed fertilizers suitable for general use or for particular crops are readily obtainable and save the amateur the time and trouble of making up his own mixtures. But a good general purpose mixture may be made of 1 part sulphate of ammonia, 2 parts superphosphate and 1 part sulphate of potash.

*Liquid manure* Many manures can be applied in liquid form. Dried blood, at 1 oz. to 2 gal. of water is commonly used as a stimulant, and a good general purpose liquid can be made from farmyard manure by suspending a quantity of manure in a strong sack in a tub of water for several days with the volume of water five or six times the volume of manure. Various proprietary liquid manures are also available and should always be used according to the maker's instructions.

Chemical fertilizers must be applied carefully as many of them may cause scorching if they fall on the leaves of plants. Lime should be applied during the winter and not be put on with other manures.

*Storing manures* All dry manures must be stored in a dry, cool place. Small quantities should be kept in boxes or barrels and large amounts delivered in sacks should rest on strips of wood and not against metal such as corrugated iron. If a manure sets or cakes, the sack should be thumped hard with a wooden mallet.

## RATES OF DRESSINGS

Farmyard manure or compost, 6–10 cwt. per 100 sq. yds.
Shoddy, spent hops, 1–2 cwt. per 100 sq. yds.
Hydrated lime, 8 oz. per sq. yd. every three or four years.
Chalk, 10–15 oz. per sq. yd. every three or four years.
Quick lime, 4–5 oz. per sq. yd. if required.
Compound or general fertilizer, 2–6 oz. per sq. yd.
Sulphate of ammonia $\frac{1}{2}$–1 oz. per sq. yd. as a top dressing.
Hoof and horn, bone, fish, meat meals, 2–4 oz. per sq. yd.
Sulphate of potash, $\frac{1}{2}$–1 oz. per sq. yd.
Superphosphate, calcium cyanamide, 1–2 oz. per sq. yd.
Basic slag, 4–6 oz. per sq. yd.

## MULCHING

A mulch is a layer of material spread over the soil to check the evaporation of moisture and reduce big changes in soil temperature. Well-decayed manure, compost, peat, chaff, etc., put on loosely about 2 in. thick are the most suitable; lawn clippings should not exceed 1 in., as they tend to pack down in wet weather. Black plastic sheeting may also be used, pegging it down along rows of vegetables or seedlings.

# 6. SOWING AND PLANTING

Among the many garden plants that are raised from seed, several require special treatment. The hardiest may safely be sown out of doors, others require some sort of protection, and still others need the artificial conditions of a heated green-house. Some of the hardy kinds are often treated as half-hardy mainly for convenience, or because the seed is valuable and expensive. In all cases thorough preparation is essential and the work must be done at the best time; not too early, nor too late. For sowing in pots or trays, or for potting up in suitable soil composts, a bench is essential, and if there is no room in the tool-shed or elsewhere, one should be made up for use in the open or made to fit over the top of the barrow, the space under-neath being used for keeping the materials handy and protected.

## SOWING IN TRAYS OR PANS

Before the sowing season begins, all boxes, pans, pots and crocks should be washed clean with an ordinary detergent and rinsed, in order to destroy the fungi which cause the fatal "damping off" of seedlings. Trays may be of wood or plastic, 2–3 in. deep, 10–16 in. long and 8–10 in. wide and provided with drainage holes or narrow spaces in the bottom. Alter-natively earthenware pans 3 in. deep and 5–10 in. in diameter, or pots not less than 5 in. in diameter may be used. They should be filled with one of the sterilized seed composts which can be bought at most shops and centres, or failing this, a second best can be made from a mixture of 2 parts loam, 1 of peat and $\frac{1}{2}$ of coarse sand. The compost should be levelled off evenly and pressed gently with a flat piece of wood of suitable size, to finish $\frac{1}{2}$ in. below the top of the box or pan, which should be watered and allowed to stand and drain for a day before sowing.

Seeds must be sown thinly and evenly, preferably in rows, $\frac{1}{2}$–1 in. apart, across the box, and covered by sprinkling with compost or sand. A home-made box sieve is often used for this purpose. A piece of glass and a sheet of brown paper should then be put on top to give the close, dark conditions suitable for germination, and the tray or pan placed in a frame or sheltered position in the garden. Excessive condensation on the underside of the glass should be wiped off daily, and as soon as the seedlings show through, the glass and paper must be removed and full light given. Watering will generally be unnecessary until this stage.

In frames ventilation should be given as soon as possible, especially during the day, and increasing the amount gradually. In frosty weather the frame should be covered at night with sacks, mats or a layer of straw. If sacks are used, they should rest on canes laid across the frame so as to form a space that will act as an insulator.

## PRICKING OUT

As soon as the seedlings are large enough to handle, they will require more room for growing and should be pricked out about 1–3 in. apart, into other boxes, a frame or sheltered border, according to the kind of plant. The soil for the boxes should be one of the specially made **potting composts** or, failing this, a home-made mixture of 7 parts loam, 3 parts peat and 2 parts sand, with a mixture of hoof and horn, superphosphate and chalk at the rate of two 2 lb. jam-jars to every cu. yd. of the compost. The seedlings must be lifted carefully, preferably with a flat plant-label, held by their leaves and planted into holes made with a short pointed stick about $\frac{1}{2}$ in. in diameter. They should be set with their lowest leaves just above the soil and be lightly firmed down with the fingers. A light watering should then be given and the boxes put back into the frame until ready for hardening off, or, if grown outside, protected from full sun for a few days.

## POTTING

Although pot-culture is generally associated with greenhouses, many plants and seedlings that do not require any artificial heat are the more successfully managed in pots, especially where a cold frame is available. In addition, cuttings can be more easily rooted and several hardy or half-hardy flowers be grown for decorative use in the home. All pots should be washed clean and, before use, should be stood in water for a short time, since dry pots will absorb considerable moisture from the soil that is put into them. Being absorbent, they must be stored in a reasonably frost-proof place during winter in order to avoid cracking.

The pots must be "crocked" with broken pieces of pot placed over the drainhole and filled with a seed-compost mixture for cuttings or a potting-compost for plants. Both mixtures should be moist enough to hold together if pressed in the hand, yet dry enough to crumble again when touched, and should be filled in a little at a time, the pot being tapped on the bench to settle the compost up to a level sufficiently high to take the roots of the plant comfortably. The size of pot must not be too big, since one of the objects of potting is to encourage root formation which occurs most readily around the inside of the pot.

For seedlings pricked out from boxes the best size of pot is 3 or $3\frac{1}{2}$ in. in diameter. The seedlings must be handled gently, the roots being kept in a ball and disturbed as little as possible. The soil should be filled in gradually and not pressed down. Watering after the seedling is set will generally firm the soil sufficiently. When the job is finished the lowest leaves of the seedling should be just above the soil and the soil should be about $\frac{1}{2}$ in. below the rim of the pot. For older plants, normally requiring larger pots, more drainage crocks and firmer potting are essential, and the soil that is filled in should be pressed down well round the sides of the pot, with a blunt-ended potting stick. The ball of roots must not be rammed with the potting stick but may be pressed gently with the thumb.

## POTTING-ON

Plants that are to remain in pots will need re-potting into larger sizes as they grow, and as soon as the roots are running completely round the inside of the pot the shift should be made. To remove the plant, place one hand over the pot with the stem between the fingers, and hold the bottom of the pot with the other hand; turn it upside-down and tap the rim gently on the bench or a block of wood. The new pot should contain more drainage material than the smaller one and the final soil-level should be 1 in. below the rim of the pot to allow adequate watering later on. The potting must be done firmly, but the ball as removed from the old pot should not be disturbed except to remove any dead roots or sour soil on the surface. If staking is necessary, one to three strong but thin sticks should be put in along or near the side of the pot and away from the ball of roots.

## HARDENING OFF

Plants raised in a greenhouse or heated frame must be gradually acclimatized to outdoor temperatures before they can safely be planted out. A cold frame is the most suitable, but a warm, open yet sheltered spot in the garden can often be made to serve almost as well, especially if wide boards are temporarily fixed up somewhat like the sides of a frame, to protect the plants from cold winds.

In frames which are used for growing plants the bed will be of soil and the trays or pots of seedlings may then be placed on the soil with the taller pots sunk if necessary. Frames used solely for hardening plants should have a bed of 2–3 in. of shingle or ashes and, as this will be at a lower level, large pots can be more easily accommodated. Trays and small pots may then have to be raised on a staging or boxes in order to keep them near enough to the light and prevent drawn, spindly growth. Whichever type of frame is used, ventilation must be given as soon as the plants are put in and steadily increased until the lights can be removed altogether, first during daytime and later, at night also.

## SOWING OUT OF DOORS

The soil of a seed-bed should be of average fertility and not too rich since that would encourage lush soft growth. Thorough cultivation and fine texture are much more important, and, as a general guide, the smaller the seed the finer the soil. Sowing should be done when the soil is moist but crumbly, not when it is wet and cold. In dry weather a good watering the day before may be necessary.

Firmness is essential; newly dug soil should be allowed time to settle before being raked down. Light soils may be consolidated by treading evenly along the drills but heavy or sticky soils should never be trodden in this way.

April is generally the busy month and, except for a few vegetable seeds such as parsnips or broad beans, sowing should not begin before mid-March. But if the garden is sheltered or in a warm district, the seeds of many hardy annual flowers and some vegetables usually sown in the spring may be put in in the autumn.

The seeds of plants which will later be transplanted should be sown in drills marked out with the line and measuring stick, and drawn out with a hoe, or, for very small seeds, pressed out with the back of a rake, the line being kept in position by placing one foot along it as the work proceeds. Annuals in flower beds and borders may be sown broadcast and raked in. Small seeds should be sown $\frac{1}{4}$ in. deep, medium-sized seeds $\frac{1}{2}$–1 in. deep, and large seeds, such as peas and beans, 2–3 in. deep. All must be sown evenly and not too thickly, and marked with labels showing the variety and date of sowing. Where birds are troublesome, wire-netting or cotton should be used.

## THINNING OR SINGLING

Plants, whether sown in their permanent positions or in drills, need thinning out in order to give every seedling its share of space and light. If this is not done, growth will be weak and spindly. Distances range from 6–12 in. according to the kind of plant, and the work may be done in two stages, first to 3 in. and later to the correct distance. The soil should be moist so that the unwanted seedlings can be pulled up easily and the remaining ones firmed down again where necessary. In dry weather a good watering should be given the day before.

With drilled seeds, the easiest way is to kneel between the rows, using one hand for thinning and the other for holding the selected seedlings in position.

## PLANTING OUT

Planting out is generally done with a trowel or sometimes a dibber. The soil must be fertile, well prepared beforehand and watered if necessary. In dry weather a good plan is to dig out all the holes required, fill them with water and allow it to drain away before any plants are put in. The holes must be large enough to take the roots of the seedlings without cramping or doubling them back, and deep enough for the plant to be at the same level as it was in the seed-bed or very slightly lower. The holes should always be set out with the line and measuring stick.

The seedlings should be lifted carefully with a fork and their seed-bed should be moist or, if necessary, watered the day before. In hot weather the seedlings should be shaded from the sun from the time they are lifted until they are put into their permanent position. The best time for the work is the evening.

Planting should be done firmly, the soil being carefully filled round the roots so as to avoid air pockets. A light watering may be given close to each plant after planting.

Larger plants, trees and shrubs should be treated in much the same way but for them a spade is the most convenient tool. The soil must be well prepared, sufficiently moist and well manured, the holes large enough, the planting done firmly and a good watering given afterwards. Many of these plants, trees and shrubs can now be bought at garden centres growing in containers, ready for planting out. This makes it possible to plant at almost any time of the year and to choose plants that are older than their normal transplanting age. Often the containers are of perishable material so that both plant and container can be planted together.

## STAKING AND TYING

Plants which need supporting must be tied or staked early in the season. The job can never be done satisfactorily once growth has been damaged by wind or allowed to straggle about.

Tall-growing herbaceous plants with few main stems, e.g. dahlias, should be tied to a single strong stake, and those with many stems, e.g. Michaelmas daisies, ringed with three or more lighter stakes or canes with green-coloured string run between them. Shorter, more slender plants look best when supported by bushy twigs set round them, with raffia or string used as required. Single-stemmed plants, e.g. gladioli, should be tied closely to canes. In all cases the supports should be long enough to reach to just below the lowest bloom but not protrude above, when they look unsightly.

Where more permanent support is required, e.g. for climbers on walls or fences, horizontal galvanized or plastic-covered wires should be provided, or the main branches can be tied in separately to nails. Raspberries and cordons should be tied to wires stretched taut between iron or wooden posts firmly set and well braced. Single trees or shrubs require strong stakes of suitable length set 2 ft. deep at planting time with a pad of sacking or rubber between the stem and the stake, or a special tree-tie may be used. All these permanent ties should be examined every year to see they are not so tight as to cause constriction or so loose as to cause chafing.

Sticks for peas must be long enough for the varieties grown and be set on both sides of the row about 3 in. away from the plants, leaning slightly outwards to prevent the crop bunching at the top or falling over. Runner beans require plain poles or canes, 7–8 ft. long, on either side of the row, one to each plant, sloping inwards to cross near the top and form a V, with other canes laid horizontally along the V and tied to make the whole secure against wind, or they may be set in fours and tied together at the top. Alternatively, strong posts may be set at each end of the row with wires stretched between at the top and bottom and stout strings tied between the wires The height above ground should not be more than 6 ft., as picking then becomes difficult.

## WATERING

Plants vary in their demand for water, but none can live

without it. Marsh-loving plants and certain vegetables such as celery need a full and constant supply; others, particularly seedlings, may easily suffer from too much and die. Rainwater is best, and every garden should have one or more tubs for collecting water from the roof of the house, or for filling with a hose from a tap. As a rule, watering is best done in the early morning.

Seeds properly sown in trays, pans or pots generally need no watering until after they grow through. Then the best way is to stand them in a shallow bath or tub and allow the water to be drawn up into the soil. Alternatively, a can with a fine rose may be used, sprinkling a little at a time. Young or low-growing plants should be watered through the open spout of a can or a hose held low down to prevent soil being washed away from the roots. Runner beans and young evergreen shrubs, especially when newly planted, benefit from overhead watering or syringing. If well-established plants need water they should have a good soaking that will last several days rather than a number of light sprinklings. Whenever possible the soil should be hoed before watering so that penetration is easier. Hoeing again the day after will help to prevent excessive evaporation. It is not only in summer that watering may have to be done; it is sometimes just as necessary in a dry spring.

## CLOCHES

Various sizes and designs are available, from the simple tent-type consisting of two sheets of glass to the more elaborate kinds which resemble glass frames or miniature greenhouses. Their main use is to give protection in the early and late parts of the year. They help to warm up the soil before sowing seeds, to protect the seedlings when through and, later, to ripen crops such as onions and tomatoes or protect autumn-sown flowers and vegetables. They are specially useful for bringing on early crops.

When placed in a row, the ends should be closed with a sheet of glass firmly held between stakes to prevent excessive draught, the glass being removed in hot weather to allow cool air to enter freely. As a rule, watering is not required, but when necessary the best way is to draw out a small trench along each side of the cloche-row and fill it with water from a can. Weeding should be done by taking the first cloche to the other end of the row and moving each one along as the work proceeds.

## FRAMES

As mentioned earlier, frames are necessary for sowing and raising certain plants and for protecting others. Many vegetable crops can also be grown for early consumption. The frame may be permanent, with the walls made of single brick or of concrete, 2–4 in. thick, or it may be portable, with walls of 1–1½ in. wood. They should be 9–18 in. high at the back and slope to 6–9 in. at the front, which should face south. Turf or banked-up soil, 4–6 in. thick, may also be used as temporary walls. All kinds are covered with a light consisting of a wooden framework with 3–6 rows of panes of glass or one large sheet as in the Dutch light. Various sizes and designs of lights are made, all suitable for private gardens, but the largest sizes should be avoided because they cannot be handled easily with one pair of hands. Double-span types are also available, but the single-span is usually preferable. The lights should be provided with wire or cord loops for securing them to the frame in order to prevent damage by wind.

Frames, whether cold or heated require daily attention, usually for a few minutes only, and great care in ventilation and watering. The most common causes of failure are too little of one, too much of the other, or allowing the glass to become dirty. Ventilation should not be done by pushing down the light, but by resting the top end on a stout block of wood measuring about 6 or 8 in. by 2–3 in. by 1 in. This gives three different openings. On hot days, the light should be removed completely.

*The cold frame* This is nothing more than a protective device suitable for housing plants which are not entirely hardy, for raising early batches of hardy seedlings, growing certain vegetables and striking cuttings. When required solely for housing plants in pots, the bed of the frame should consist of a 2–3 in. layer of shingle or ashes, but if seeds are to be sown or

46

vegetables grown, it should be made up of 6 in. of soil on a layer of garden compost, and after settling should be 8–12 in. from the glass.

*Heated frames* Few private gardeners use the old type of hot bed consisting of a frame placed on a layer of fermenting manure which provides sufficient warmth to last for two or three months, the temperature dropping slowly but steadily all the time. Today, heated frames generally depend on electricity which may be installed as small space heaters round the inside of the frame or as warming cables buried in the soil. Both types are perfectly satisfactory and allow a number of tender plants and a wide range of cuttings to be raised.

# 7. WHAT TO GROW

Deciding what to grow is never an easy matter. The choice is wide and new varieties are continually being added, while the soil, situation and size of the garden set their own limits. In a new garden it is better to start off with a small selection of plants and place them boldly with plenty of room for each than to crowd in too many or attempt to have something of everything. And until experience and knowledge have been gained, or some group of plants has been chosen for specialization, it is better to keep to the proved varieties which are known to do well on most soils and in most parts of the country. Selections of such plants are given below under their common and generic names. There are many others, and many named varieties, and every year something new comes on offer.

## ANNUALS

Annuals offer a wide range of colour and a long period of flowering extending from May to October, the majority blooming in July and August. Height varies from a few inches to 7 ft. (sunflowers), the general run being from 1 ft.–3 ft. Many are available as mixtures, strains or named varieties of known colours and a few, such as antirrhinums and petunias, may be bought as first-generation or "$F_1$" hybrids which are generally more vigorous and more colourful.

## HARDY ANNUALS

For sowing during April and May, generally where required to bloom, and thinned.

| COMMON NAME | GENERIC NAME | COMMON NAME | GENERIC NAME |
|---|---|---|---|
| Californian Bluebell | Nemophila | Californian Poppy | Eschscholzia |

48

**A colourful border. In the foreground are delicate
petunias and in the background striking red cannas.**

An informal garden with a real feeling of peacefulness.
Such a garden is within the capabilities of the beginner.

| | | | |
|---|---|---|---|
| Candytuft | Iberis | Night-scented Stock | Matthiola |
| Clarkia | Clarkia | Scarlet Flax | Linum |
| Coreopsis | Coreopsis (annual) | Shirley Poppy | Papaver |
| Cornflower | Centaurea | Sunflower | Helianthus |
| Corn Marigold | Chrysanthemum (annual) | Sweet Alyssum | Alyssum (annual) |
| Godetia | Godetia | Sweet Sultan | Centaurea |
| Larkspur | Delphinium | Toad Flax | Linaria |
| Love-in-a-Mist | Nigella | Virginia Stock | Malcomia |
| Marigold | Calendula | | |
| Mignonette | Reseda | | |
| Nasturtium | Tropæolum | | |

## HALF HARDY ANNUALS

For sowing in trays, in a frame or in a sheltered border in April, pricked out or transplanted, hardened off and put in their flowering positions end of May or early June. Can also be bought ready for planting out.

| COMMON NAME | GENERIC NAME | COMMON NAME | GENERIC NAME |
|---|---|---|---|
| African Marigold | Tagetes | Indian Pink | Dianthus (annual) |
| Ageratum | Ageratum | Lobelia | Lobelia |
| Annual Phlox | Phlox drummondii | Love-lies-bleeding | Amaranthus |
| Canary Creeper | Tropæolum | Nemesia | Nemesia |
| China Aster | Callisthephus | Petunia | Petunia |
| Cockscomb | Celosia | Purslane | Portulaca |
| Cosmea | Cosmos | Salpiglossis | Salpiglossis |
| Everlasting Flowers | Helichrysum | Salvia | Salvia |
| French Marigold | Tagetes | Snapdragon | Antirrhinum |
| Gaillardia | Gaillardia | Statice | Limonium |
| | | Sweet Scabious | Scabiosa |
| | | Ten-week Stock | Matthiola |

| Tobacco Plant | Nicotiana | Verbena | Verbena |
|---|---|---|---|
| | | Zinnia | Zinnia |

## BIENNIALS

For sowing out of doors during summer, thinned or transplanted when large enough and put into permanent positions in autumn or spring for flowering in the following summer. (Certain perennials, e.g. gaillardia, hollyhock, are best treated as biennials.)

| COMMON NAME | GENERIC NAME | COMMON NAME | GENERIC NAME |
|---|---|---|---|
| Canterbury Bell | Campanula | Iceland Poppy | Papaver |
| Evening Primrose | Oenothera | Mullein | Verbascum |
| Forget-me-not | Myosotis | Stock, Brompton Intermediate, Lothian | Matthiola |
| Foxglove | Digitalis | | |
| Gaillardia | Gaillardia | Sweet William | Dianthus |
| Hollyhock | Althaea | Wallflower | Cheiranthus |
| Honesty | Lunaria | | |

## PERENNIALS FOR HERBACEOUS BORDERS

To be planted in autumn or spring, preferably in autumn, dwarfs 8 to 12 in. apart, medium heights 12 to 18 in. and tall plants 2 to $2\frac{1}{2}$ ft. apart. Plant in bold groups according to height, with some late-flowering sorts level with or slightly in front of early-flowering ones of the same height. Plant firmly, with roots well spread out; label. Keep borders free from weeds, stake and tie in good time, fork in a little manure or compost every spring or dress with complete fertilizer 2 to 4 oz. per sq. yd. Remake every five years. (To obtain the full range of colours, heights and flowering season given below, it will generally be necessary to grow more than one species or variety of each.)

| COMMON NAME | GENERIC NAME | COLOUR | HEIGHT (ft.) | SEASON |
|---|---|---|---|---|
| Anchusa | Anchusa | Blue | 2-5 | May-July |

## Herbaceous plants

| | | | | |
|---|---|---|---|---|
| Astilbe | Astilbe | White, pink, red | 1-3 | June-Aug. |
| Bellflower | Campanula | White, blue | 1-3 | June-July |
| Bergamot | Monarda | Red, purple | 2-3 | July-Sept. |
| Blazing Star | Liatris | Purple | 2 | July-Sept. |
| Bleeding Heart | Dicentra | White, pink, red | 2-3 | July-Sept. |
| | | | 1 | June |
| Campion | Lychnis | White, red | 1-3 | June-Aug. |
| Carnation | Dianthus | Various | 1-1½ | June-Aug. |
| Catmint | Nepeta | Lavender | 1-1½ | June-Sept. |
| Centaurea | Centaurea | Various | 2-4 | June-Aug. |
| Chamomile | Anthemis | Yellow, gold | 1-2 | July-Aug. |
| Chinese Lantern | Physalis | White | 1-2 | July |
| Chrysanthe-mum (border) | Chrysanthe-mum | Various | 2-4 | July-Oct. |
| Cinquefoil | Potentilla | Yellow, red | 1-2 | June-Aug. |
| Columbine | Aquilegia | Various | 1-2 | May-July |
| Coneflower | Rudbeckia | Yellow, orange | 2-4 | July-Sept. |
| | Echinacea | Purple | 3-5 | July-Sept. |
| Coral Bells | Heuchera | Red | 1-2 | June-July |
| Coreopsis | Coreopsis | Yellow, bronze | 1-3 | June-Sept. |
| Cranesbill | Geranium | Various | 1-3 | June-Sept. |
| Daisy | Bellis | White, pink, red | ½-1 | Apr.-June |
| Day Lily | Hemero-callis | Orange, red | 2-4 | July-Aug. |
| Delphinium | Delphinium | White, blue, mauve | 3-5 | June-Aug. |
| Doronicum | Doronicum | Yellow | 2-3 | Apr.-June |
| Erigeron | Erigeron | Blue, orange, pink | 1-2 | June-Aug. |
| Evening Primrose | Oenothera | White, yellow | 1-3 | July-Aug. |
| Flag | Iris | Various | 2-3 | May-July |
| Geum | Geum | Yellow, red, orange | 2 | May-Sept. |
| Globe Flower | Trollius | Yellow, orange | 2-3 | May-June |
| Globe Thistle | Echinops | White, blue | 3-5 | July-Aug. |
| Goats Rue | Galega | White, blue, pink | 3-4 | June-Sept. |

| | | | | |
|---|---|---|---|---|
| Golden Rod | Solidago | Yellow | 2-5 | Aug.-Sept. |
| Gypsophila | Gypsophila | White, pink | 2-3 | June-Sept. |
| Helenium | Helenium | Yellow, red, orange | 2-5 | June-Sept. |
| Incarvillea | Incarvillea | Rose | 1-1½ | June |
| Knapweed | Centaurea | Pink, blue, purple | 1-2 | June-Aug. |
| London Pride | Saxifraga | Pink | 1-1½ | May-July |
| Loosestrife | Lysimachia | Yellow | 2-3 | June-Aug. |
| | Lythrum | Purple | 2-4 | July-Aug. |
| Lupin | Lupinus | Various | 2-3 | June-July |
| Marguerite | Chrysanthemum | White | 2-3 | June-Sept. |
| Megasea | Bergenia | Pink, red | 1 | Apr.-June |
| Michaelmas Daisy | Aster | Various | 1-6 | Aug.-Sept. |
| Monkshood | Aconitum | Blue, white | 3-5 | June-Sept. |
| Musk | Mimulus | Yellow, brown, orange | 1½-1 | June-Aug. |
| Paeony | Paeonia | White, pink, red | 2-3 | June-July |
| Phlox | Phlox | Various | 2-4 | July-Sept. |
| Pink | Dianthus | Various | 1-1½ | June-Aug. |
| Plantain | Hosta | White, lilac | 2 | June-Aug. |
| Poppy Lily | Papaver | White, pink, red | 2-4 | May-Aug. |
| Pyrethrum | Chrysanthemum coccineum | White, pink, red | 2 | May-July |
| Red-hot Poker | Kniphofia | Red, yellow | 3-5 | June-Sept. |
| Sage | Salvia | Blue, purple | 2-4 | July-Aug. |
| Scabious | Scabiosa | White, mauve, blue | 2-4 | July-Aug. |
| Shasta Daisy | Chrysanthemum | White | 2-3 | July-Sept. |
| Sidalcea | Sidalcea | White, rose, red | 2-4 | July-Aug. |
| Solomon's Seal | Polygonatum | White | 2-4 | June-July |
| Sunflower | Helianthus | Yellow, red, gold | 5-8 | Aug.-Oct. |
| Thrift | Armeria | Pink, white | ½-1 | May-July |
| Tibetan Poppy | Mecanopsis | Blue | 2-3 | July-Aug. |

| Turtle Head | Chelone | Rose | 1-2 | Aug. |
|---|---|---|---|---|
| Valerian | Kentranthus | White, red | 2-3 | June-July |
| Veronica | Veronica | White, blue, red | 1-4 | June-Sept. |
| Viola | Viola | Various | ½ | May-Oct. |
| Wind Flower | Anemone | White, pink, mauve | 2-4 | Aug.-Sept. |
| Woundwort | Stachys | Rose, violet, | 1-2 | June-July |
| Yarrow | Achillea | White, pink, yellow | 2-4 | June-Aug. |

# PLANTS FOR ROCK GARDENS AND WALLS

| COMMON NAME | GENERIC NAME | COMMON NAME | GENERIC NAME |
|---|---|---|---|
| Aubrieta | Aubrieta | Sandwort | Arenaria |
| Auricula | Primula | Saxifrage | Saxifraga |
| Bellflower | Campanula (dwarf) | Soapwort | Saponaria |
|  |  | Stonecrop | Sedum |
| Cinquefoil | Potentilla | Sun Rose | Helianthemum |
| Draba | Draba | Thrift | Armeria |
| Flax | Linum | Thyme | Thymus |
| Gentian | Gentiana | Valerian | Kentranthus |
| Gromwell | Lithospermum | Viola | Viola |
| Houseleek | Sempervivum | Windflower | Anemone (herbaceous) |
| Phlox | Phlox (dwarf) |  |  |
| Pinks | Dianthus | Yarrow | Achillea (dwarf) |
| Primula | Primula |  |  |
| Rock Cress | Arabis | Yellow Alyssum | Alyssum |

BULBS Allium, anemone, chionodoxa, crocus, fritillary, iris, muscari, narcissus, scilla, snowdrop, tulip.

SHRUBS Brooms, cotoneaster, heaths; and dwarf types of cypress, cedar, juniper and yew.

In addition, many annuals may be used. Snapdragons and wallflowers are specially suited to dry walls and, once established, usually continue to seed themselves.

## WATER PLANTS

| COMMON NAME | GENERIC NAME | COMMON NAME | GENERIC NAME |
|---|---|---|---|
| Arrow Head | Sagittaria | Reed Mace | Typha |
| Bog Arum | Calla | Reeds | Arundo |
| Cape Pond Weed | Aponogeton | Sweet Flag | Acorus |
| Flag | Iris | Water Lily | Nymphaea |
| Marsh Marigold | Caltha | Water Violet | Hottonia |

Oxygenators: Ceratophyllum, Elodea

## ORNAMENTAL TREES OR SHRUBS

To be planted in autumn or spring, well watered, and staked as necessary. The small selection below is restricted to those generally suited to the average-sized garden and gives the height and spread in feet of the more popular varieties. To obtain a rough idea of the distance for planting in a mixed shrubbery take the average spread of the two shrubs chosen to grow next to each other, add together and divide by two. The tall or large kinds should only be chosen where there is plenty of room, and shade and root-spread will not interfere with other plants. Many choice species require special soil conditions. Rhododendrons, for example, require a lime-free soil while others such as choisya, cistus and pittosporum are not fully hardy and therefore not generally suitable. Local nurserymen will always be ready to advise in specific cases.

| COMMON NAME | GENERIC NAME | DECIDUOUS or EVERGREEN | HEIGHT ft. (according to species) | SPREAD ft. |
|---|---|---|---|---|
| Acacia | Robinia | D | 10-30 | 15-30 |
| *Azalea | Rhododendron | D, E | 3-10 | 2-8 |
| *Berberis | Berberis | D, E | 2-12 | 3-12 |
| Bachelor's Buttons | Kerria | D | 3-10 | Continuous |
| Blue Spiraea | Caryopteris | D | 4-5 | 4-5 |
| Broom | Cytisus, Genista | D, E | 4-12 | 3-12 |
| Buddleia | Buddleia | D | 10-20 | 10-18 |

## Trees and shrubs

| | | | | |
|---|---|---|---|---|
| †Ceanothus | Ceanothus | D, E | 10-20 | 8-12 |
| †*Cotoneas-ter | Cotoneaster | D, E | 2-20 | 2-12 |
| Crab | Malus | D | 20-25 | 20-25 |
| *Daphne | Daphne | D, E | 3-5 | 2-6 |
| *Deutzia | Deutzia | D | 3-10 | 4-8 |
| Dogwood | Cornus | D | 6-20 | 8-20 |
| Elaeagnus | Elaeagnus | D, E | 5-10 | 5-10 |
| †Escallonia | Escallonia | D, E | 4-12 | 5-12 |
| Flowering Almond | Prunus | D | 4-20 | 5-20 |
| Cherry | Prunus | D | 10-40 | 10-30 |
| Plum | Prunus | D | 15-25 | 15-30 |
| * Currant | Ribes | D | 6-10 | 8-12 |
| †*Golden Bell | Forsythia | D | 5-12 | 5-12 |
| Gorse | Ulex | E | 5-7 | 5-7 |
| *Guelder Rose | Viburnum | D | 3-15 | 10-15 |
| *Heaths | Erica | E | 1-10 | 2-3 |
| Hibiscus | Hibiscus | D | 5-10 | 5-10 |
| †Honey-suckle | Lonicera | D | 6-9 | 6-10 |
| *Hydrangea | Hydrangea | D | 4-8 | 6-9 |
| †*Japonica | Chaeno-meles | D | 3-12 | 3-12 |
| Laburnum | Laburnum | D | 18-30 | 15-30 |
| Laurestinus | Viburnum | E | 7-10 | 4-15 |
| Lavender | Lavandula | E | 1-4 | 1-4 |
| Leycesteria | Leycesteria | D | 5-8 | 2-4 |
| Lilac | Syringa | D | 6-20 | 6-20 |
| Magnolia | Magnolia | D, E | 10-30 | 10-30 |
| Mahonia | Mahonia | E | 3-5 | Continuous |
| Maple | Acer | D | 10-20 | 10-15 |
| May | Crataegus | D | 10-20 | 15-20 |
| Mexican Orange | Choisya | E | 5-8 | 5-6 |
| Mountain Ash | Sorbus | D | 10-30 | 20-30 |
| †*Myrtle | Myrtus | E | 8-10 | 8-10 |
| Pieris | Pieris | E | 5-8 | 5-10 |
| †*Pyracantha | Pyracantha | E | 10-18 | 12-18 |
| *Rhododen-dron | Rhododen-dron | E | 2-15 | 3-15 |
| Rock Rose | Cistus | E | 2-8 | 3-8 |
| Senecio | Senecio | E | 3-4 | 3-6 |

| | | | | |
|---|---|---|---|---|
| Skimmia | Skimmia | E | 3-4 | 3-5 |
| *Snowberry | Symphori-carpus | D | 6-8 | 8-12 |
| Snowy Mespilus | Amelanchier | D | 10-20 | 10-15 |
| Spindle | Euonymus | D | 5-7 | 5-10 |
| *Spiraea | Spiraea | D | 3-10 | 3-8 |
| *St. John's Wort | Hypericum | D | 1-5 | 1-6 |
| Strawberry Tree | Arbutus | E | 15-20 | 10-15 |
| Sumach | Rhus | D | 10-15 | 8-15 |
| *Syringa | Philadelphus | D | 6-12 | 6-15 |
| Tamarisk | Tamarix | D | 5-7 | 5-7 |
| Veronica | Hebe | E | 1-6 | 2-9 |
| Viburnum | Viburnum | D | 5-10 | 5-12 |
| *Weigela | Weigela | D | 4-10 | 4-9 |
| Wych Hazel | Hamamelis | D | 7-12 | 5-7 |

\* Will succeed in partial shade. For full shade use box, laurels, mahonia, privet, hypericum, holly.

† Suitable for growing against walls.

## WEEPING TREES

Weeping species of many kinds of trees and shrubs can also be obtained. Among those that flower, the most suitable for gardens are forsythia, may, crab and Japanese cherry. Others such as ash, beech, birch, Mountain ash and willow require considerable space.

## CONIFERS

Great care is necessary when choosing conifers for an average-sized garden. Unless there is plenty of room, an acre or more, the tall-growing kinds which reach a height of 40–50 ft. or more must be avoided. Their rate of growth is usually fairly slow, but once they have got beyond the gardener's reach and become too large it is an expensive business to have them removed, and only a very few will stand lopping or heading back. All kinds look best as single trees forming a special feature. They should be planted in October or April and well watered. If drying winds follow, further watering will be necessary.

Most species of cedar, cypress, fir, larch, spruce and pine are tall trees. Those of more suitable height are:

| | |
|---|---|
| Chamaecyparis lawsoniana *var* albo spicata | 15-20 ft. |
| Chamaecyparis lawsoniana *var* fletcheri | 8-12 ft. |
| Chamaecyparis lawsoniana *var* pottenii | 12-15 ft. |
| Cupressus macrocarpa aurea | 20-30 ft. |
| Golden and Irish Yew | 10-15 ft. |
| Juniper | 5-15 ft. |
| Thuja dolabrata | 15-20 ft. |

*Dwarf conifers* Dwarf species, mostly cypresses, junipers spruces and thujas, are also obtainable, their maximum heights ranging from 1 to 5 ft. They are particularly suitable for rock gardens and tubs, or for planting in specially constructed positions on terraces.

## CLIMBING PLANTS

Plants suitable for walls, fences or pergolas need careful attention, particularly in their early years. The holes for planting should be dug out 2 ft. deep and at least 2 ft square, and manure or compost forked in at the bottom. If the soil has been spoilt by building it must be taken out and replaced. The plants should be set 6–9 in. from the wall or pillar and well watered. Further watering will be necessary in the early years; it should always be a good soaking and never a light surface sprinkling, since the roots must be encouraged to go down to the natural water-level and not stay in the surface soil, where they may easily dry out.

In addition to the shrubs marked † on page 55, clematis, everlasting pea, jasmine, polygonum, climbing and rambler roses, vines and wisteria may be chosen. They are suitable for the following aspects:

ANY ASPECTS: Clematis, cotoneaster, forsythia, honeysuckle, japonica (chaenomeles), jasmine, polygonum, pyracantha, vine.
SOUTH or WEST: Ceanothus, escallonia, everlasting pea, magnolia, myrtle, roses, solanum, wisteria.

## ROSES

No garden can be complete without roses but the choice of varieties needs careful consideration, particularly if space is limited. The range is now so wide, with new varieties being added every year. The first step is to study a good catalogue and then to visit the nursery during the flowering season. Climbers and ramblers may be planted as single specimens but for bedding it is invariably better to have, say, four or six bushes of only a few separate varieties than single specimens of twelve or more varieties. In areas where black spot is troublesome, it is most important to choose only those varieties that are resistant to the disease. All types of roses should be planted in the same way as other shrubs and pruned and sprayed as advised in Chapters 9 and 11.

## BULBS

Bulbs require a good, well-drained soil. Most of them may be left down for several years before being taken up, divided and replanted, but tulips, gladioli, and hyacinths should be lifted every year after the leaves have died down, dried, and stored in a cool, airy place.

### PLANTING TABLE

| | DEPTH (in.) | DISTANCE APART (in.) | TIME OF YEAR |
|---|---|---|---|
| Aconite | 2-3 | 2-3 | Oct. |
| Allium | 3 | 3 | Sept.-Oct. |
| Anemone | 2-3 | 4-6 | Oct.-Apr. |
| Chionodoxa | 2-3 | 3 | Sept.-Dec. |
| Colchicum | 2-4 | 3-6 | Aug. |
| Crocus | 3-4 | 2 | Sept. |
| Daffodil | 4-6 | 6 | Sept.-Oct. |
| Fritillary | 4 | 4-6 | Oct. |
| Gladiolus | 4 | 9 | Mar.-Apr. |
| Hyacinth | 4-6 | 9 | Sept.-Nov. |
| Iris | 3-4 | 6 | Sept.-Oct. |
| Montbretia | 2-3 | 3-4 | Feb.-Mar. |
| Muscari | 2-3 | 2-3 | Oct. |
| Ranunculus | 2-3 | 3-4 | Mar. |

| | | | |
|---|---|---|---|
| Scilla (inc. Bluebell) | 3 | 3-4 | Sept.-Oct. |
| Snowdrop | 3-4 | 3 | Sept.-Nov. |
| Tulip | 4-6 | 6 | Oct.-Nov. |

*Bulbs in bowls* The best results come from buying selected or "prepared" bulbs, and good quality fibre. The fibre must be well soaked and allowed to drain before being used and the bulbs planted so that their tips show just above the finished surface. The bowls should then be put in a dark, cool place and watered as necessary, without getting the fibre sodden. Any excess moisture can be drained off by tipping the bowl on its side, using one hand to keep the fibre in position.

When the shoots are about 1 in. long, the bowls should be brought into partial light for a few days, then into full light, but still kept cool. When the flower-buds can be seen, the bowls may be put into a warm room, preferably not above 65° F., and turned daily so that all the shoots get equal light.

## FRUIT

All kinds of fruit require plenty of room and an open but not exposed situation. For the average-sized garden, trees should be of the bush or pyramid type or where space is very limited the choice should be confined to cordons and trained trees. All of these are raised on selected dwarfing stocks. Standard trees on vigorous-rooting stocks are suitable only for the larger garden or where a single specimen may be used as a special feature. Protection from birds and wasps is often difficult or even impossible, especially with cherries, pears, plums and peaches. In spring birds will strip the wood buds as well as the fruit buds with the result that the tree can neither make normal growth nor produce fruit, and begins to look unsightly with long lengths of bare branches showing where the buds have been taken. Soft fruits are generally more suitable for a small garden and may be grown under a permanent wire-netting cage, 8 ft. high, or fish-netting put on a temporary structure. Wasps' nests must be found and destroyed.

*Planting* Fruit should be planted in the autumn or early spring, preferably the autumn, but in either case the soil must be in good condition. Strawberry runners should be planted as soon as they are well rooted, those raised in pots often being ready by the end of July. Trees should be staked at the time of planting.

Since soft fruits and the dwarf types of tree fruits are surface rooting, deep cultivation is impossible after planting. The soil must therefore be thoroughly prepared, deeply dug and well manured beforehand.

## PLANTING DISTANCES

| Apples, pears | Standard | 20-30 ft. | Bush | 10-15 ft. |
|---|---|---|---|---|
| | Half-standard | 15-20 ft. | Espalier | 12-15 ft. |
| Cherries | | 30 ft. | | |
| Plums | | 15 ft. | | |
| Cordons | | 2 ft. | Rows 6-8 ft. apart | |
| Currants, gooseberries | | 5 ft. | ,, 5 ft. ,, | |
| Loganberries, blackberries | | 8-10 ft. | ,, 8 ft. ,, | |
| Raspberries | | 2 ft. | ,, 6 ft. ,, | |
| Strawberries | | 15-18 in. | ,, 2½ ft. ,, | |

*Cultivation* Except for well-established trees growing happily in a lawn or grass orchard, fruit must be cultivated regularly but shallowly, and, particularly in the case of the soft fruits, kept free from weeds. Pruning and spraying must be carried out as required (see Chapters 9 and 11), and cordons, trained trees and young bushes should be mulched in early summer. After June, when many fruitlets normally drop, it may be necessary to thin apples, pears and plums, giving each fruit a space equal to the width of a hand, and to prop branches carrying heavy crops.

*Manuring* As a general rule, soft fruits require complete and liberal manuring every year, but tree fruits need more particular treatment. Young trees require nitrogen in their early years while forming the main framework of branches, but afterwards, potash and phosphates are more necessary to help fruit formation and ripening. Too much nitrogen leads to excessive growth of wood and for this reason it is generally unwise to grow fruit trees among vegetables which require a good supply. Farmyard manure should be applied in the autumn, fertilizers in early spring. The long-lasting organic fertilizers are generally best for the soft fruits.

## SUITABLE DRESSINGS (per sq. yd.)

| | |
|---|---|
| Apples | ⎤ Sulphate of potash 1-2 oz., Superphosphate |
| | ⎟    1-2 oz. |
| Pears | ⎦ Sulphate of ammonia 1 oz. if growth is weak. |
| Plums | ⎱ As above, plus hydrated lime 4 oz. every 3-5 |
| Cherries | ⎰    years. |
| Peaches | Sulphate of potash 1-2 oz. Bone meal 4 oz. |
| Red currants | ⎤ Farmyard manure or compost lightly forked |
| Gooseberries | ⎟    in. Sulphate of potash 1-2 oz. Bone meal |
| | ⎦    4 oz. |
| Black currants | ⎤ Farmyard manure or compost lightly forked |
| Raspberries | ⎟    in. Sulphate of potash 1-2 oz. Bone meal |
| Loganberries | ⎟    or hoof and horn 4 oz. Sulphate of am- |
| Strawberries | ⎦    monia 1 oz. after fruiting. |

*Choosing Varieties* Before fruits can "set" and grow they must be fertilized with pollen. Many are self-fertile and can use their own pollen, but others such as the sweet cherries and certain apples, pears and plums are self-sterile and must receive pollen from other distinct varieties, while a few must have pollen from certain specific varieties only. In all cases the flowers must open over the same period; an early-flowering variety cannot be fertilized by a very late-flowering variety. In choosing self-sterile varieties, special care must therefore be taken to provide a pollinator and to select one of the same flowering period. The wisest course is to seek advice from a nursery specializing in fruit trees but a provisional choice may be made from the following which are generally suitable for most districts.

### APPLES

| NAME | DESSERT or COOKING | SEASON | TYPE of TREE | FLOWERING PERIOD |
|---|---|---|---|---|
| *Arthur Turner | C | July-Oct. | Bush | Mid-season |
| Blenheim Orange | D, C | Nov.-Feb. | Standard | Late |
| Bramley's Seedling | C | Nov.-Apr. | Standard | Mid-season |

61

| | | | | |
|---|---|---|---|---|
| *Charles Ross | C, D | Oct.-Nov. | Bush | Mid-late |
| Cox's Orange Pippin | D | Nov.-Jan. | Bush, cordon | Early |
| Early Victoria | C | July-Aug. | Bush | Mid-season |
| *Edward VII | C | Dec.-Apr. | Standard | Late |
| Ellison's Orange | D | Oct. | Bush, cordon | Mid-season |
| *James Grieve | D | Sept.-Oct. | Bush, cordon | Early |
| Lane's Prince Albert | C | Nov.-Mar. | Bush | Mid-season |
| Newton Wonder | C, D | Nov.-Mar. | Standard, bush | Late |
| Ribston Pippin | D | Nov.-Jan. | Bush | Early |
| *Worcester Pearmain | D | Sept.-Oct. | Bush | Early |

\* Self-fertile.

## PEARS

| NAME | DESSERT or COOKING | SEASON | TYPE of TREE | FLOWERING PERIOD |
|---|---|---|---|---|
| Beurré Hardy | D | Oct. | Bush | Mid-season |
| *Conference | D | Oct.-Nov. | Cordon, bush | Early |
| Doyenné du Comice | D | Nov. | Cordon, wall | Late |
| Louise Bonne of Jersey | D | Oct. | Bush | Early |
| *William's Bon Chrétien | D | Sept. | Bush, standard | Late |

\* Self-fertile.

## CHERRIES

Only the Morello is self-fertile. Sweet cherries need cross-pollinating, so at least two must be planted together and few gardens can provide sufficient space. The most generally suitable combination is Napoleon or Early Rivers (black) with Waterloo.

## PLUMS

| NAME | DESSERT or COOKING | SEASON | TYPE of TREE | COLOUR of FRUIT |
|------|------|------|------|------|
| Cambridge Gage | D | Aug. | Half-standard | Golden green |
| Czar | C | Aug. | Half-standard | Purple |
| Denniston's Superb | D | Aug. | Half-standard | Golden yellow |
| Early Transparent | D | Aug. | Half-standard | Golden yellow |
| Marjorie's Seedling | C | Sept.-Oct. | Half-standard | Blue |
| Oullin's Golden Gage | D | Aug. | Half-standard wall | Yellow |
| Purple Pershore | C | Aug. | Half-standard | Purple |
| Victoria | D, C | Aug. | Half-standard wall | Red |

**All are self-fertile.**

*Damsons.* Merryweather or Shropshire Prune.

## CURRANTS

| *Black* | | *Red* | |
|------|------|------|------|
| Baldwin | Late | Laxton's No. 1 | Early |
| Boskoop Giant | Early | Red Lake | Mid-season |
| French Black | Mid-season | Wilson's Long Bunch | Late |
| Wellington XXX | Early | | |

*White*
White Versailles

## GOOSEBERRIES

| Whinham's Industry | C | Red | Mid-season |
|------|------|------|------|
| Golden Drop | D | Yellow | Mid-season |
| Leveller | D | Yellow | Mid-season |
| Whitesmith | C | Green-yellow | Mid-season |

## STRAWBERRIES

| *Early* | *Mid-season* | *Autumn Fruiting* |
|------|------|------|
| Cambridge Favourite | Redgauntlet | Red Rich |
| | Royal Sovereign | Sans Rivale |

## CANE FRUITS

| *Blackberries* | *Loganberries* | *Raspberries* |
|---|---|---|
| Parsley-leaved | Thornless | Lloyd George |
| John Innes | | Malling Promise |

## OTHER FRUITS

*Apricots, Figs, Grapes, Nectarines and Peaches* can be grown success-fully in warm, sheltered districts, preferably on a south wall. Peaches may also succeed as bush trees. It is essential to choose "outdoor" varieties such as:

| Apricots | Breda, Moor Park |
|---|---|
| Figs | Brown Turkey, Brunswick |
| Grapes | Black Cluster (black), Royal Muscadine (white) |
| Nectarines | Lord Napier |
| Peaches | Hale's Early, Peregrine |

## VEGETABLES

The most suitable soil is a deep medium loam of good texture, well drained yet retentive of moisture, thoroughly cultivated and liberally manured. Lighter and heavier soils will also pro-duce excellent crops of many kinds, but the gardener should aim at getting his soil as near the ideal as possible, for the object is to grow a heavy weight of high-quality produce from a small area. Six well-grown, full-sized cauliflowers are of far greater use than a dozen little ones.

Where space is limited, the less bulky crops, e.g. salads, and those which occupy the ground for a short time and can be followed by a second crop, e.g. early peas, should be chosen. If there is room for more they should be grown to a set plan or rotation, since this enables the best use to be made of the fertilizers and plant food in the soil, makes cultivation easier and helps to control diseases and pests.

*Rotations* After reserving space for the permanent crops such as herbs, rhubarb, sea-kale or asparagus, the main portion of the vegetable garden should be divided into three plots of approximately the same size and cropped as follows:

A border of
spiraea, 'Anthony
Waterer'. This
variety flowers
in early spring.

A spray of lilac, 'Clarks Giant'. There are a good
many garden varieties of this shrub to select from.

Thuja, a pyramidal cedar, is an excellent evergreen tree and makes an attractive feature in a small garden.

|  | PLOT 1 | PLOT 2 | PLOT 3 |
|---|---|---|---|
| 1st year | Leguminous Crops (peas, beans) | Brassica Crops (cabbage, sprouts, cauliflower, kale, etc.) | Root Crops (beetroot, carrots, celery, leeks, etc.) |
| 2nd Year | Brassica Crops | Root Crops | Leguminous Crops |
| 3rd Year | Root Crops | Leguminous Crops | Brassica Crops |

*Catch cropping* Quick-growing crops such as early carrot, lettuce and radish can be sown from the end of March to mid-April between rows of beans, on the banks of the celery trench or any space reserved for late-planted crops. Late lettuce, spinach and spinach-beet may follow early peas, and winter cauliflower or spring cabbage follow early potatoes.

*Choosing varieties* Different varieties suit different districts, and the wisest course is to be guided by the local seedsman. In buying early varieties for quick maturity it is essential to choose those which have been bred for the purpose and not to use main crop varieties which have been bred for their long growing season. The following are suitable for warm sheltered borders, cold frames or cloches:

Lettuce: May Queen, All the Year Round
Carrot: Early Gem, Early Horn
Radish: French Breakfast
Turnip: White Milan, Early White Frame

## SOWING AND PLANTING TABLE (for outdoors)

| CROP | TIME to SOW | TIME to PLANT or TRANS-PLANT | DISTANCE BETWEEN ROWS | PLANTS | PERIOD OF USE |
|---|---|---|---|---|---|
| Artichoke (Jerusalem) | — | Feb.-Mar. | 2½-3 ft. | 1 ft. | Nov.-Mar. |
| Asparagus | Apr. | Apr. | 1-1½ ft. | 1 ft. | May-June |
| Beans | Nov. or | — | 2 ft. | 6 in. | June-Aug. |
| Broad | Feb.-Mar. | | | | |
| French | Apr.-May | — | 2 ft. | 9 in. | July-Aug. |
| Runner | May-June | May | 4-6 ft. | 9 in. | July-Oct. |
| Beetroot | Apr.-June | — | 1 ft. | 4-6 in. | All year |
| Broccoli (Sprouting) | Apr.-May | June-July | 2 ft. | 2 ft. | Feb.-May |

E

| | | | | | |
|---|---|---|---|---|---|
| **Brussels Sprouts** | Mar. | May | 2½ ft. | 2 ft. | Nov.-Mar. |
| **Cabbage** | | | | | |
| Spring | Aug. | Sept. | 1½ ft. | 1½ ft. | Mar.-May |
| Summer | Apr. | May | 2 ft. | 2 ft. | June-Aug. |
| Autumn | Apr.-May | June | 2 ft. | 2 ft. | Sept.-Oct. |
| Winter | May | July | 2 ft. | 2 ft. | Nov.-Jan. |
| **Carrot** | | | | | |
| Early | Mar.-Apr. | — | 1 ft. | 3 in. | June-Aug. |
| Main | May | — | | 6 in. | Sept.-May |
| **Cauliflower** | | | | | |
| Summer | Mar.-Apr. | Apr.-June | 2 ft. | 2 ft. | July-Sept. |
| Autumn | Apr.-May | June | 2 ft. | 2 ft. | Oct.-Nov. |
| Winter | Apr.-May | July | 2 ft. | 2 ft. | Dec.-May |
| **Celeriac** | Mar.-Apr. | May-June | 1½ ft. | 1 ft. | Oct.-Mar. |
| **Celery** | Apr. | May-June | 3 ft-(trench) | 9 in. | Oct.-Feb. |
| **Celery, Self-blanching** | Apr. | May-June | 1 ft. | 9 in. | Aug.-Oct. |
| **Chicory** | May-June | — | 1 ft. | 9 in. | Oct.-Apr. |
| **Corn Salad** | Feb.-Aug. | — | 1 ft. | 6 in. | All year |
| **Cress** | Mar.-Sept. | — | In pots, or boxes | | Mar.-Sept. |
| **Endive** | May-Aug. | — | 1 ft. | 1 ft. | Oct.-Feb. |
| **Kale** | Apr.-June | June-July | 2 ft. | 2 ft. | Nov.-Mar. |
| **Kohl-rabi** | Apr.-May | May-June | 2 ft. | 1 ft. | July-Nov. |
| **Leeks** | Mar. | May-June | 1 ft. | 9 in. | Nov.-Mar. |
| **Lettuce** | | | | | |
| Summer | Mar.-July | Apr.-May | 1 ft. | 9 in. | May-Oct. |
| Winter | Aug.-Sept. | Oct. | 1 ft. | 6 in. | Apr.-May |
| **Marrow** | May | May-June | 3-4 ft. | 3-4 ft. | July-Nov. |
| **Onion** | Mar. or Aug. | Apr. | 1 ft. | 6 in. | All year |
| „  (sets) | — | Mar. | 1 ft. | 6 in. | Aug.-Apr. |
| **Parsnip** | Feb.-Mar. | — | 1-1½ ft. | 6-9 in. | Nov.-Mar. |
| **Peas** | | | | | |
| Early | Mar.-Apr. | — | 2½ ft. | 3 in. | June-July |
| Main | Apr.-May | — | 3-3½ ft. | 3 in. | July-Aug. |
| **Potatoes** | | | | | |
| Early | — | Mar. | 2 ft. | 12-15 in. | June-Oct. |
| Main | — | Apr.-May | 2½ ft. | 15 in. | Oct.-May |
| **Radishes** | Mar.-Sept. | — | 1 ft. | 1-2 in. | Apr.-Sept. |
| **Rhubarb** | — | Mar. | 3 ft. | 3 ft. | Apr.-Aug. |
| **Salsify** | Apr.-May | — | 1 ft. | 9 in. | Oct.-Mar. |
| **Savoy** | Apr.-May | June-July | 2 ft. | 2 ft. | Oct.-Mar. |
| **Sea-kale** | — | Mar. | 1½ ft. | 1½ ft. | Feb.-Apr. |
| **Scorzonera** | Apr.-May | — | 1 ft. | 9 in. | Oct.-Mar. |
| **Sea-kale Beet** | Apr.-May or Aug. | — | 1 ft. | 9 in. | June-Oct. Apr.-May |
| **Shallots** | — | Feb.-Mar. | 1 ft. | 6 in. | July-Mar. |
| **Spinach** | | | | | |
| Summer | Mar.-May | — | 1 ft. | 6 in. | June-May |
| Winter | Aug.-Sept. | — | 1 ft. | 6 in. | June-May |
| **Spinach Beet** | Apr.-May or Aug. | — | 1 ft. | 9 in. | June-Oct. Apr.-May |
| **Swedes** | June | — | 1 ft. | 9 in. | Oct.-Mar. |
| **Tomatoes** | — | May-June | 2 ft. | 1½ ft. | Aug.-Oct. |
| **Turnips** | Mar.-June | — | 1 ft. | 9 in. | June-Nov. |
| Tops | July-Aug. | — | 1 ft. | 3 in. | Mar.-May |

*Manuring* If available, farmyard manure or compost should be used for brassicas, potatoes, leeks and celery, but not for roots such as carrots or parsnips which are then inclined to "fork". Failing these manures, use long-lasting organics, e.g. bone meal or hoof-and-horn with potash, and top-dress as required with sulphate of ammonia. Never top-dress winter vegetables, e.g. sprouts, cauliflowers, after July, as this encourages sappy growth. Give heavy-feeding crops such as celery and leeks, liquid manure regularly throughout summer. Lime plots in turn every three or six years.

*Special Cultural Notes* (For general notes on Sowing, Thinning, Planting, Watering, etc., see Chapter 6.)

*Celery* Plant 9 in. apart in a trench 18 in. deep and 12 in. wide prepared well in advance, and having 6–8 in. of manure or compost in the bottom covered with fine soil. As plants grow, earth-up carefully with soil from the banks. A paper "collar" may first be put round the stems if preferred. Self-blanching celery, if well grown, does not need earthing-up.

*Cos Lettuce* Blanch by tying the leaves together at the top.

*Endive* Blanch by covering with a box or inverted flower-pot with the hole filled up.

*Leeks* Drop into holes 9 in. deep and 3 in. in diameter, and allow rain and subsequent watering to fill in the soil.

*Peas and Beans* If sticks are unobtainable, grow dwarf varieties of peas, and pinch out growing points of runner beans to form a bush.

*Potatoes* Plant 4–5 in. deep in trenches or holes. Earth-up two or three times during season as stems grow.

*Rhubarb* For early supply, cover with forcing pots or boxes January–February. Remove by May. Cease pulling after July. Never pull newly planted roots the first season.

*Sea-kale* Cover as rhubarb in November or December. After cutting, remove pots and allow to grow naturally.

## HERBS

Herbs take up little space, since one or two bushes of the perennial kinds and a short row of the annuals are sufficient for most needs. An average soil and a fairly sunny position are required. The following are generally suitable:

| NAME | PROPAGATION | DISTANCE for PLANTING or SINGLING | USE |
|---|---|---|---|
| *a* Basil | Sow Apr.-May | 1 ft. | Soup, sauce Dry for winter |
| *a* Borage | Sow Apr.-May | 1 ft. | Beverages |
| Chives | Divide Mar. or Oct. | 6 in. | Salad, soup Cut regularly |
| Garlic | Plant bulbs Mar. 2in. deep | 9 in. | Harvest in Aug. and store |
| Horse-radish | Set root cuttings Mar. in raised beds 2 ft. high | 1 ft. | Sauce |
| *a* Marjoram | Sow Mar.-Apr. | 9 in. | Soup, stew Dry for winter |
| Mint | Divide roots Oct. or Mar. Renew bed every 3 years | 1 ft. | Sauce, vegetables |
| *a* Parsley | Sow Apr. and July Slow to germinate | 6 in. | Sauce, garnish |
| Sage | Cuttings Apr. or sow Apr.-May | 2 ft. | Stuffing Dry for winter |
| Thyme | Sow or take cuttings Apr.-May | 9 in. | Stuffing Dry for winter |

*a* = annual or best treated as annual.

# 8. PROPAGATION

As distinct from seed-sowing, there are several vegetative methods by which many plants can be multiplied. The advantages are that the plants can often be raised more quickly, and since many garden plants are hybrids which do not breed true from seed, they form the only sure way of reproducing exact replicas of the parent.

## CUTTINGS

Various types of cuttings are used for propagating bushes, shrubs and herbaceous plants. The hardy kinds can be rooted out of doors in a cool spot protected from full sun and drying winds; the less hardy require the protection and closer atmosphere of a frame, bell-jar or cloche, while the more tender kinds need artificial warmth and in many cases a special propagating frame inside a heated greenhouse. All require moist conditions and protection against drying out from the time they are taken off the parent plant. Every preparation must therefore be made beforehand. Out of doors, the bed must be dug over a few days previously, watered if necessary and, except on light soils, coarse sand mixed in. For the less hardy cuttings to be set in pots, boxes or a frame, a prepared compost should be bought and for the more shy-rooting kinds, a proprietary rooting hormone should be used.

*Stem Cuttings* Sound, well-grown shoots of the current year's growth should be selected, cut off and prepared as follows:

*Hard-wood Cuttings* Late summer or early autumn is generally the best time. Select a shoot, preferably from the lower but outside part of the plant, 12 in. long, and, if possible, cut with a "heel" or slice of the older branch from which it is growing. Trim the edges of the heel and if the tip of the shoot

69

looks soft and unripened, cut it off to the second or third bud.
If no heel is taken, cut the shoot just below a joint or bud. All
cuts must be clean and sharp. Next, remove the leaves from the
lower half or two-thirds of the cutting and, if the new plant
will be required to grow on a stem or "leg" and not to produce
new sucker-like growth from below soil level, remove the lower
buds also.

Take out a short trench with a trowel or spade and set the
cuttings 6–9 in. apart, with half or slightly more of their length
below ground level. Replace the soil carefully and fairly firmly,
making sure that the bottom of the cutting rests on soil and that
there are no air pockets; water, and afterwards keep the soil
moist but not wet. Never plant a cutting by pushing it into the
soil, as this may easily open or strip the bark at the cut end.
Rooting generally takes 1–6 months, occasionally longer, according to the kind of plant. Transplanting can therefore be
done the following spring or autumn.

*Soft-wood and herbaceous cuttings* During spring and
early summer cuttings can be taken from the new growth of
many shrubs and herbaceous plants, e.g. lupin, dahlia,
chrysanthemum. A frame or glass covering, such as a bell-jar or
cloche, and pots or boxes filled with mixed compost are
necessary. Make the cuttings 3–6 in. long and cut just below a
leaf-joint, using a razor blade for the softer tissues. Remove the
leaves from the lower half, and plant so that $\frac{1}{3}$ to $\frac{1}{2}$ of the cutting
is below the surface, using a wooden plant label as a dibber and
as a lever to firm the soil around the base. According to size,
plant 1–3 in. apart or put three or four in a 5 in. pot, planting
them round the edge where they root more readily. Give a good
watering and put in a frame or under glass, away from sunshine. Do everything possible to prevent drying out at any
stage, but avoid overcrowding and getting the soil too wet, as
fungus rots may then develop. The cuttings should not touch
each other closely and their lowest leaves should not lie flat on
the soil.

Rooting normally takes 3–6 weeks and is shown by the
turgid appearance of the leaves and the beginning of new
growth. Ventilation must then be given, and soon after, the
cuttings should be potted-up, or hardened off and planted out.

*Root cuttings* can be taken of a number of fleshy-rooted plants, e.g. anchusa, oriental poppy, sea-kale, rhubarb, etc. The best time is early spring when the buds or eyes on the root show up as small whitish pimples. Cuttings may be 2–6 in. long but each must contain an eye. Trim the top, i.e. the end nearer to the main stem, level, and the other end slanting, so as to avoid any risk of the cuttings being planted the wrong way up. Plant with the top 1 in. below the surface. Water and transplant in autumn or following spring.

## LAYERS

Many shrubs, climbing and herbaceous plants can be layered during summer, generally July. Some, such as honeysuckle and loganberry, will root readily if the tip of a stem is bent over, pegged down to some soil which has been forked over, and covered with a little mound of soil. With others, such as carnations, veronica, laurel and some rhododendrons, the shoot must first be slit on the underside beneath a joint, making the cut 1–3 in. long, extending from the outside to the centre. Turn the end of the shoot upwards to open the "tongue" of the slit and peg down on to forked-over soil, placing the peg between the cut and the main stem. Cover with 1–4 in. of soil and water lightly. Carnations should root in 2 or 3 months, shrubs 3–12 months.

## RUNNERS

A few plants, e.g. strawberries, send out runners which form leaves at their joints and root readily in loose soil, or can be pegged down on pots filled with a suitable compost. When the roots have formed, the stem connecting with the parent is cut and the young plant repotted or transplanted.

## ROOT DIVISION

A large number of herbaceous plants and many shrubs can also be increased by division in autumn or spring. The work deserves more attention than is generally given. Each "clump" should be lifted carefully and the roots separated gently or cut clean with a sharp knife. With most herbaceous plants, the best young roots are on the outside; the centre is the oldest and should be thrown away. Some, such as polyanthus, and several rock plants, form a number of separate "crowns" or complete new plants, which should be disentangled gently.

## OFFSETS

Offsets may be either a form of runner, e.g. sempervivum (houseleek) and some of the stonecrops, or small young bulbs formed from the parent, e.g. daffodil. If planted in nursery rows they will grow on to flowering-size in 2–4 years according to their kind.

## BUDDING

Many woody plants, particularly roses, fruit trees and ornamental trees are normally propagated by budding. By this process, varieties which do not root as cuttings or, if they do, form poor or unsuitable root systems, can be put on to a more common or more robust species which is easily and quickly multiplied. The stock must, however, be of the same or a closely related species. The chief advantage is that weak-growing varieties can be budded on to strong-rooting stocks and over-vigorous varieties on to dwarfing stocks, making both types more suitable for garden use.

Budding is usually done on young stocks 1–2 years old, when they are as thick as a pencil or a little more, but it can also be used for repairing damage to young trees or to fill in bare spaces in a trained tree. A budding-knife with a sharp blade and a handle tapering to a thin flat wedge, and some raffia are necessary. The best time is from the end of June to the beginning of September, when the sap is flowing well, and, since the work must be done quickly and the buds not allowed to dry out, everything must be made ready beforehand.

To obtain the bud of the variety required, cut off a good length of well-grown outside shoot with well-developed wood-buds. If it has to be brought any distance, e.g. from a friend's

## FIGURE 7

A wood-bud of the desired variety has been cut out with a shallow slice of the bud-shoot, and it is shown from 1, the front, and 2, the rear view. The T cut in the stock, 3, is made at, or just below soil level. The bud is neatly slipped into the stock, 4, and the sides of the T carefully smoothed.

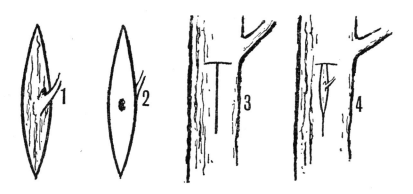

garden, put it in a jar with a little water or wrap it in damp paper or moss. To prepare the stock, brush away any mud splashed up on the lowest few inches and at 2–3 in. from ground level and on the north side make a horizontal cut about $\frac{1}{2}$ in. long through the soft bark down to, but not into the hard wood. From the centre of this make a similar cut vertically downwards, about 1 in. long, to form a T. On rose stocks the T should be made at soil level or just below and the loose soil around the stock should be brushed away beforehand.

Then, holding "the bud-shoot" by the top end with the lower end away from the body, select one of the middle buds, cut off the leaf, but leave the leaf-stalk to act as a handle, and cut out the bud with a shallow slice beginning $\frac{1}{2}$ in. below and finishing $\frac{1}{4}$ in. to 1 in. above the bud. Holding the bud by its "handle", prise out with the point of the knife the small piece of wood found immediately under the bud. If the base of the bud comes away as well, leaving an obvious depression, the bud is ruined and another try must be made, or a new bud cut more thinly when the tiny piece of wood left in will not matter.

Next, using the handle of the knife, open the T on the stock

73

and, holding the bud by its leaf stem, slip it under the bark on both sides down to the bottom of the slit. Smooth the sides of the T carefully with the fingers and cut off any part of the insertion coming above the T. Tie firmly with raffia above and below the bud, and after a month or so examine the tie. If too tight, slit the tie at the back of the stock. The bud will normally begin to grow the following spring, when the stock should be cut back to just above it, or a few inches may be left until late summer to act as a support for the new growth to be tied to. As the new shoot grows longer, it should be tied to a cane. If growth begins in the first autumn, the stock should be cut back then to within 6 in. of the bud and levelled off in the spring. All side-growths and any suckers from the stock must be removed.

## GRAFTING

Grafting is used for the same general purpose as budding and again, the two individual plants must be of the same or nearly related species. It is particularly useful for repairing serious damage, for renovating old but healthy trees, or for adding another variety on to one or two branches of an established tree to improve or effect pollination. It is also used on leafy and tender plants, but considerable skill, special propagating frames and heated greenhouses are necessary. The principle is the same as in budding, and depends upon the union of the cambium or growing layer between the bark and the wood of the two plants, but the difference is that, instead of a bud, a short piece of shoot called a scion is used. The work is done in spring when the sap is beginning to rise in the stock but since it is essential for the scions to be in a more dormant state than the stock, they are cut off the chosen variety in autumn and heeled into the soil in a shaded place. There are several methods of grafting, but only three or four are likely to be of use to the private gardener.

*Whip and tongue grafting* is most suitable when the stock and scion are roughly the same size, about $\frac{1}{2}$ in. in diameter. Cut the stock back to 6 in. from the ground with a sloping cut and make a vertical slit in the middle of this slope.

74

Then take out from the middle of the stored scion a portion having four buds, the lower end being cut with a slope to match that of the scion and finishing $\frac{3}{4}$ in. below a bud, the top end being cut almost level above the top bud. Make a slit upwards in the lower end of the scion to provide a tongue to match the slit on the stock, and fit the two together, making sure that the bark meets along one side if not both. Tie with raffia and cover with grafting wax. Remove any basal growth from the stock.

*Saddle grafting* is used for slightly larger stocks which are cut back to a point with two sloping but unequal sides. The scion is cut to match, so that at least a part of one side fits exactly.

*Crown or rind grafting* is used where the stock is larger than the scion and is particularly valuable in renovating old trees. In January or February saw off the branches of the tree that is to be grafted to about 2 ft. from the trunk or main stem. In April saw off another 2 in., smooth with a knife and cut a vertical slit in the bark about 3 in. long, one on a branch up to 3 in. diameter, two on a 4 in. branch and three on a 6 in. branch. Prepare the scion, cutting the lower end in the form of a thinly tapering wedge about 2 in. long, to fit the slits. Tie with raffia and wax. When growth begins, allow some shoots to come from the stock until the grafts are strong, then remove.

*Stub grafting* is also used for renovation, the stock tree being cut back more lightly to leave branches about 1 in. in diameter. On each of these, an oblique cut about $\frac{1}{2}$ in. deep is made on the top side near the main branch. This is opened by bending the shoot down, and a wedge-shaped scion cut with one side of the wedge 1 in. long, the other $\frac{1}{2}$ in., is slipped in and waxed. The branch is then cut back. No tying is necessary.

*Bridge grafting* is specially suited for repairing serious damage such as may be caused by rabbits or machines. The bark of the trunk is trimmed back above and below the damaged area and a slit made in each. A scion or shoot is cut to span the distance, each end being pointed and slipped in under the bark, tied and waxed. Two or three such scions may be necessary. The buds on the "bridge" should be rubbed out.

75

# 9. PRUNING

The object of pruning is to shape a bush or tree into the form desired and to arrange its branches in the way best suited for flowering or fruiting. Pruning generally encourages the production of more branches, and for this reason young trees and shrubs are usually pruned hard in their first few years until a good framework has been obtained. Later, they are pruned more lightly or scarcely at all, those that flower on young wood being pruned sufficiently to ensure a succession of new growth, while those that flower on older wood are pruned mainly to keep them in proper shape and free from overcrowding. Overvigorous growth, particularly in fruit trees, cannot be checked by hard pruning which merely results in yet more new growth, especially if the real reason is a very rich soil or too much nitrogen. On the other hand, weak growth can often be stimulated by pruning.

## HOW TO PRUNE

A knife, secateurs, long-arm pruner and saw, preferably a pruning saw with curved blade and pistol-handle, are usually required. All must be of good quality, sharp and in good condition, because clean cuts heal naturally and quickly, whereas rough, jagged cuts heal poorly and often allow fungus diseases to enter. Secateurs should not be used on soft growth which can be cut easily with a knife, because bruising or pinching may result. All cuts should be made to an outside bud pointing in the direction which the new growth is desired to take, slanting slightly upwards towards the bud and ending just above it. If too low the bud will be damaged; if too high a dead snag will be left.

Where a whole branch has to be removed, it must be cut off close to the main branch or trunk to leave no snag. If the branch is large and heavy, the underside should be sawn through into the hard wood and the weight supported so that the branch does not fall and strip the bark below the cut. Saw cuts should be pared off smooth with a knife to assist healing, and all large cut surfaces should be painted over with grafting wax.

*Ornamental trees and shrubs* As a general guide ornamental trees and shrubs should be allowed to grow to their natural shapes, pruning being used mainly to help early formation, remove poor, weak growth, prevent overcrowding and take out old branches to make room for new shoots.

*Flowering trees* In their first year almonds, crabs, laburnum, etc., should be pruned to form a good framework in much the same way as a fruit tree. Subsequently little pruning is needed beyond thinning and removing weak growth. All suckers must be cut out.

*Flowering shrubs* should be pruned soon after flowering, particularly those that flower in late winter and early spring, e.g. forsythias. Only summer- and autumn-flowering kinds should be left until the winter, e.g. purple buddleia.

*Evergreens and conifers* require little or no pruning, except when grown as a hedge or topiary specimen. April is the best time for evergreens, early autumn for conifers. Single specimen trees should be allowed to grow naturally with only light trimming where necessary.

# ROSES

*Newly planted trees and bushes* planted in the autumn should be pruned the following March or April and those planted in spring pruned at planting time, bushes being cut back to 4–6 in., ramblers and climbers to about half their length and standards to 6–8 in. from the union at the top of the stem. Weak or badly placed stems should be cut out.

*Established trees and bushes* During March or earlier if more convenient, the stems of bush roses should be cut back to 4–6 buds, the centre being kept open and free from crossing or in-growing shoots; dwarf polyanthas should be pruned fairly hard, the taller varieties only lightly. Species and shrub roses should merely be thinned as required. Climbers and

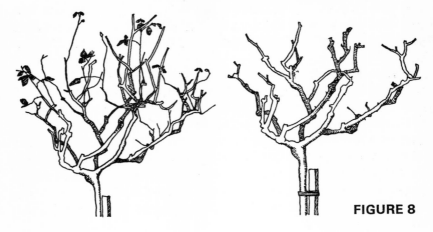

**FIGURE 8**

ramblers should be pruned after flowering, the climbers requiring little more than thinning or spacing, and re-tying. Ramblers should have the oldest wood cut out at ground level and the new shoots trained-in in its place. Except where a rose has been raised from a cutting and is growing on its own roots, all suckers must be regularly removed.

## FRUIT

The main pruning of fruit trees should be done during the late winter and finished in early spring by the time the buds show signs of swelling. The chief object is to keep all branches well spaced and, in the case of bush or standard trees, to keep the centre open and free from in-growing branches. Newly planted trees should have their main branches cut back to $\frac{1}{2}$ or $\frac{1}{3}$ of their length, and any long side shoots shortened to four or five buds. In the following year the pruning should be much lighter, the leading shoots being merely tipped or cut back more where a new branch is wanted. Once the shape and the number of main branches are as required, the system of pruning varies according to the kind of fruit and type of tree.

*Summer pruning* Cordons and wall-trained trees should have the current season's side-shoots pinched back to about

78

six leaves during July or August in order to check growth and let in sunshine, but leaders must not be stopped at this time of year. Peaches, nectarines and Morello cherries which fruit on this new growth the next season must not be summer-pruned. (See later.)

*Apples and pears* In winter the side shoots of dwarf trees should be cut back to four or five buds and on cordons and other trained trees to two or three buds. The leading shoots of each main branch should be tipped lightly. Weak-growing varieties should be pruned harder, and vigorous varieties as little as necessary. Established bush trees and standards need only thinning and keeping open, which is often better done by removing one or two whole branches than by attempting to shorten several smaller ones. All cuts must be made to a wood bud, i.e. the narrow-pointed type, not the more rounded, plump type that produces blossom. Established bush and standard trees need no summer pruning. *Bark ringing* will often induce a poor-cropping but otherwise healthy tree to produce fruit. A strip of bark about ½ in. wide is removed from the trunk in two half-rings, one about 3 or 4 in. above the other. The work should be done in late spring when the sap is rising strongly, and the cuts covered with grafting wax.

*Cherries and plums* Once the tree has been formed, pruning should be as light as possible. Hard pruning encourages "gumming" and sometimes disease. Wall-trained plums may require summer pruning.

*Morello cherries* New growth must be taken in to replace the old. In early summer select three new growths on each of the previous season's shoots, at the base, middle and top. Pinch out all others. In winter cut back the old shoot to the selected new basal growth which is used to replace it, or to the middle growth if there is room for this to grow as well.

*Peaches and nectarines* Winter pruning is the same as for Morello cherries. In early summer new shoots are selected as required to replace the older fruiting shoots, all surplus shoots being removed or disbudded. Disbudding should be done gradually at intervals, not all at once.

*Black currants* Newly planted bushes should be cut back to two or three buds above ground level. In subsequent winters the oldest shoots which have fruited should be cut down to ground level wherever new shoots have grown to take their place, or cut back to where new side-growth has developed.

*Red and white currants* In winter all side shoots should be cut back to three or four buds and leading shoots tipped lightly.

*Gooseberries* The main object is to keep the bush open. All weak and in-growing branches and suckers should be removed in winter. Vigorous leaders should be cut back to three-quarters of their lengths.

*Raspberries, loganberries, blackberries* Newly planted canes should be cut back to 1 ft. high. In later years the old canes should be cut off at ground level after fruiting and the best new growth trained in. Tall-growing varieties should be tipped lightly in February, not earlier.

*Neglected Trees* Unless too old or diseased, neglected trees can often be quickly improved by opening the centre, cutting out wrongly placed or crossing branches, suckers, etc. If the tree is not making much growth, all the necessary pruning may be done during the winter at one operation, but if growth is reasonably vigorous it should be spread over two or three years, otherwise too much new growth will be stimulated. If old fruiting branches of apples and pears are overcrowded with fruiting spurs, alternate ones should be removed flush with a saw or chisel, and where strong, healthy, young shoots grow without any side shoots and the buds remain dormant, new shoots can usually be stimulated by making a cut down to the wood just above a bud.

A double-flowered almond, a magnificent
flowering tree for the small garden.

Two varieties of
deutzia. Both
flower in late
spring and are
profuse bloomers

# 10. HARVESTING AND STORING

By harvesting at the best times and storing in the correct way all kinds of garden produce can be made to last longer, and stocks of certain plants preserved for the following year.

## HARVESTING

*Fruit* Early non-keeping culinary fruit such as cooking apples and plums should be started on as soon as large enough. This will reduce waste if the crop is heavy, and if it is light will prevent birds and wasps having most of it. Other fruit should not be gathered until it is ripe, nor left till over-mature. Soft fruits should be well-coloured and tree fruits come away easily with the stalk attached. Apples and pears for eating and storing should not be picked until they can be lifted off without any pulling or twisting, and since many varieties ripen over a period they should be picked as ready. Windfalls and premature colouring may be caused by insect attacks and are no guide to ripeness. All fruit must be handled carefully because slight bruises or even finger-nail marks may allow certain organisms to enter and develop rots during storage. Picking baskets should be lined, or canvas bags used.

*Flowers* Picking should be done in the early morning and when the flowers are nearing their full opening or, in the case of spikes, e.g. gladioli, when one-third to one-half of the blooms are open. The cut flowers should then be stood in water deep enough to come up near the lowest bloom. After an hour or so they should be taken out and the stems broken off, not cut, to the length desired. Everlasting flowers, e.g. helichrysum, should be picked well before the blooms are fully open and hung up to dry, head downwards, in a cool, airy place.

Many flowering shrubs and trees, e.g. almonds, forsythia,

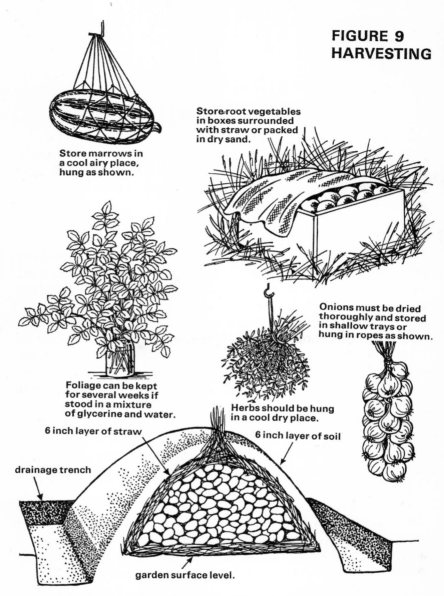

**FIGURE 9
HARVESTING**

Store marrows in a cool airy place, hung as shown.

Store root vegetables in boxes surrounded with straw or packed in dry sand.

Onions must be dried thoroughly and stored in shallow trays or hung in ropes as shown.

Foliage can be kept for several weeks if stood in a mixture of glycerine and water.

Herbs should be hung in a cool dry place.

6 inch layer of straw

6 inch layer of soil

drainage trench

garden surface level.

Storing large quantities of root vegetables and potatoes outside in heaps.

can be brought indoors for early flowering. The shoots should be cut off cleanly as soon as the buds begin to swell, and with the ends broken, stood in water in full light in a warm but not hot room.

The flowering period of most plants can be prolonged if the dying blooms are cut off, e.g. Canterbury Bells will produce a second crop, violas will continue for most of the summer and dahlias bloom until frost comes.

Bulbs and dormant roots of plants must be properly air-dried before storing, the separate varieties being put into trays or shallow boxes and labelled. Roots of half-hardy plants such as dahlias must be stored in a frost-proof place. If there is any doubt about the insulation, they should be put into boxes well covered round with straw.

*Vegetables* Crops grown purposely for early use should be started on as soon as they are large enough and have developed their flavour. Main crops, and those that keep throughout the winter, should be left until full-grown. Many vegetables, e.g. leeks, parsnips and salsify, may safely be left in the soil, although a little straw should be laid over them in very severe weather. Turnips should also be left, since those that are not used will produce "tops" early the following year. Other kinds must be stored and protected from wet and frost. Onions should be harvested in August, well dried and stored in shallow trays or tied together to form a "rope". Carrots and beetroot should be lifted during October, the tops twisted off, and stored in boxes or barrels. Main-crop potatoes should be harvested as soon as the tops have died down and stored in the dark.

*Herbs* Many herbs, such as mint, sage, thyme and marjoram can be dried for winter use. They should be harvested in late summer or early autumn, tied into small bunches and hung in a cool, airy place until thoroughly dry. Drying in artificial heat reduces their flavours.

# THE STORE-ROOM

Few gardens are equipped with a proper store-room and most gardeners have to make do with a part of the tool-shed, an attic, cellar or garage. These can be used successfully if they are reasonably dry and well ventilated, dark, free from draughts, rats and mice, have a fairly constant temperature and can be made frost-proof. The greatest disadvantage is a fluctuating temperature; it should be between 30°–40° F. and not exceed 50° F. For this reason attics and garages are not usually suitable, but if a garage must be used, the store-corner should be at ground level and away from the car radiator. For fruit, a slightly humid atmosphere is beneficial, and a shed with an earth floor or built partly below ground is most suitable.

If there is no ventilation, a brick may be knocked out or several holes bored close to the roof of a wooden shed, and a wooden flap made for fitting over the opening in severe weather. Frost-proofing is best done with a 6-in. layer of straw put on the floor and wrapped round the stacks of trays or boxes as they are brought into the store. Polythene sheets should not be used, because they may prevent proper circulation of air. Everything must be arranged for regular examination and only sound, unblemished fruit and roots should be stored.

For the first two weeks, the store should be ventilated as much as possible, and the fruit and vegetables left uncovered at the top. After this initial "sweating" long-keeping fruit should be wrapped in oiled wraps.

## SEEDS

Seed-saving is a specialist's job, and as a general rule it is far better for the gardener to buy seed every year than to risk the dangers of cross-pollination and seed diseases or the effects of unsuitable drying and storage facilities. But certain flower seeds, chiefly the annuals, and a few vegetables such as peas and beans can often be saved satisfactorily. The plants must be left growing until the seeds are fully ripe (by which time they generally look unsightly) and harvesting done by picking the pods or seed-heads complete. These should be spread on newspaper, dried at room temperature, then separated from the pods and chaff and put into bottles or tins and labelled. Seed saved from plants that are normally increased vegetatively, e.g. herbaceous perennials, will invariably lead to disappointment. They do not often breed true and the chance of getting a new and better variety is most unlikely.

*Seed potatoes* These are not true seeds, but vegetative parts of the plant, and must be stored in a frost-proof place. They should be arranged "eye-end" up in shallow trays and given full light to encourage short, sturdy shoots. As a general rule, seed potatoes should not be saved from garden crops because of the incidence of virus diseases.

# 11. HEALTH AND DISEASE

There is nothing more disheartening to a gardener than to see a crop spoilt by disease after it has received proper care and attention during the growing season. Fortunately, modern research has shown how to prevent or control most diseases and pests provided the right action is taken at the proper time. Delay makes control difficult and eradication impossible, and may lead to complete loss. The gardener must therefore get to know the common diseases and be able to recognize the early symptoms.

For convenience, the word disease is here used to cover all forms of ill-health in plants whether caused by bacteria, fungi, viruses, physiological disorder, insects or other lower animals. Bacteria, viruses, many fungi and a few insects generally cause disease inside the plant, while other fungi and the majority of insects occur on the outside. Bacteria multiply by simple cell-division and with the viruses, are usually spread by some external agent such as a sucking insect, the gardener's hands or tools, or occasionally on seeds. Fungi grow somewhat like an ordinary plant, having a vegetative stage and a fruiting stage producing "seeds" (spores) which may be easily spread by wind. Insects generally go through four stages of development, egg, larva or grub, pupa or chrysalis and adult, the last being the most infective when the females generally fly about to lay their eggs and so start new infestations on other plants.

*Control measures* Much can be done by good, careful and tidy gardening. A plant that is growing happily is less liable to disease or more capable of growing away from it, careful handling and pruning will reduce infection through bruises and wounds, and general tidiness will remove many common breeding grounds. The washing of pots and boxes, clearing weeds from hedgerows, regular hoeing and the proper use of a bonfire and compost heap all help considerably, and every encouragement should be given to the gardener's natural

86

friends. Birds generally do more good than harm, especially if netting and cotton are used where necessary; hedgehogs, toads and shrewmice eat a great variety of pests, while many ground beetles, the well-known ladybirds, centipedes, the aptly named hover-flies and beautiful lacewing all live on other insects. Earthworms are entirely beneficial, but may be a nuisance on lawns.

Usually, however, more direct measures such as spraying and dusting are necessary. Leaf-eating insects can be destroyed by coating a poison onto their food, but sucking insects must be covered with a substance that will destroy their own tissue or asphyxiate them. Both can be killed by "systemic" insecticides which are absorbed by the sap. Surface fungi can be controlled by spraying or dusting at most times of the year, but the deep-seated kinds can, as a rule, only be dealt with successfully during their fruiting stage. For the more persistent of them, and for most of the virus and bacterial diseases, the surest and, in the end, often the cheapest way in gardens, may be to cut the loss, grub and burn the ailing plants.

The spray or dust to be used and the time of application will vary according to the kind of disease, its position on the plant, the method of attack and spread, and the most vulnerable stage. The choice is nowadays a simple matter since many efficient, ready-to-use proprietary brands are available and the gardener is able to buy as necessary. But the following should always be on hand:

*A general insecticide*, harmless to all plants.
*Green Sulphur* or general "surface" fungicide.
*A slug-killer* based on *Metaldehyde* ("Meta").

*Warning* Many sprays and dusts are poisonous and must be handled with great care; when not in use they should be locked away out of the reach of children and pets. The maker's instructions must be followed carefully, particularly those giving the dosage or listing any plants for which the specific product may not be suitable. Fruit and ornamental trees should not be sprayed when in full blossom owing to the danger to bees and other pollinating insects. Winter spraying with tar oils should not be done on trees if vegetables or plants are growing underneath. Spraying should not be done in windy weather; it is generally ineffective and may harm plants in the neighbouring garden. Derris should not be used close to ornamental ponds or streams because they are poisonous to fish.

## GENERAL DISEASES

Common on many kinds of trees, shrubs, flowers, fruit and vegetables:

*Ants* do not themselves attack plants, but their workings are unsightly on lawns and paths, and may smother seedlings or upset the roots. They also "nurse" aphids and frequently carry them from one plant to another.

Destroy the nests with boiling water, paraffin, liquid derris or a proprietary ant-killer. If the nest cannot be found, sprinkle a little sugar and watch the ants carry it away.

*Aphids,* the well-known greenfly or blackfly; may also be white, reddish or blue-tinted. Sometimes found on roots as well as leaves and stems; usually exude a sticky substance over the foliage on which black moulds grow.

Spray or dust with malathion, derris or BHC.

*Capsid bugs,* green or reddish brown, $\frac{1}{3}$ in. long, cause rusty-looking pin-prick holes in the leaves and damage the growing point, often making it fork.

Spray with malathion. Covering also the soil around the plants as the insects drop off readily when approached.

*Centipedes* unlike Millepedes (q.v.) are beneficial, have one pair of legs to each body segment, which is generally flat, not round, and run away when disturbed.

*Chafer beetles* The grubs are fleshy, curved, white with brown heads, and feed on plant roots, often causing a sudden wilting.

Dig up and destroy, or trap in pieces of turf placed grass downwards.

*Cuckoo spit* is the white froth surrounding a small, pale greenish-yellow grub, usually found on stems.

Spray forcibly with malathion or pick off by hand.

*Cutworms* are grey to black caterpillars feeding at or just below ground level at night. Plants wilt or may be cut right through.

Collect and destroy or dust around plants with BHC.

*Damping off* is generally confined to seedlings growing in frames or under glass and is due to several fungi causing the stems to collapse at soil level.

Use sterilized soil; avoid excessive moisture; ventilate. Water with Cheshunt Compound or proprietary captan or copper spray.

*Earwigs* feed at night particularly on greenhouse plants and dahlias, generally hiding during daytime.

Keep the borders tidy; dust with BHC or trap in pieces of sacking, crumpled paper or straw.

*Eelworms* are minute, only the largest visible. They live in soil and in many plants; cause stunted, malformed growth and premature leaf-drop.

No cure; destroy infested plants and grow a non-related group.

*Flea beetles* attack seedlings which look "blue"; small holes appear in the leaves.

Spray or dust with derris or BHC; clear up rubbish.

*Leaf miners* The larvae of several species live in the tissue of leaves and make characteristic tunnels.

Spray with malathion or BHC or squash the miners with finger and thumb.

*Leaf spots,* generally round and brownish, are caused by several different fungi.

Use proprietary copper spray.

*Leather jackets,* the dirty, greyish legless grubs of the Daddy Longlegs, up to $1\frac{1}{2}$ in. long, feed on plant roots and may cause sudden wilting. Generally only serious in neglected gardens or after breaking up old turf.

Dust with BHC.

*Mildew* may be the surface Powdery Mildew causing a whitish or greyish effect, or the deeper type of Downy Mildew generally causing yellowish patches on the leaves with a greyish or purplish downy growth on the underside. Shoots of trees may wither.

For Powdery Mildew, dust with sulphur and remove infected shoots; for Downy Mildew remove infected shoots or plants if badly attacked and use a copper-lime spray or dust.

*Millepedes* differ from *Centipedes* in being cylindrical with two pairs of legs to each body segment and generally curl up when disturbed. As a rule they do not attack plants but extend the damage caused by wounds or other insects.

Dust seedlings with BHC or trap in pieces of carrot or potato.

*Red spider* occurs as grey or red mites in webs on the undersides of leaves, making them look dry, rusty or silvery.

Spray with malathion or derris.

*Rusts* cause small brown, reddish or orange-coloured spots on leaves.

Remove infected leaves as soon as seen; in bad cases burn plants.

*Rots* due to fungi or bacteria often enter through wounds or bruises, especially on crops in store. They may be wet or dry; stem-rots also occur, causing a sudden wilting, or a dry canker.

Remove and burn infected plants.

*Sawflies or Slugworms* The larvae of some sawflies resemble caterpillars while others look like small slugs. They feed on shoots and leaves, often eating away the surface or rolling the leaves up.

Spray with BHC and hoe soil underneath to kill the pupae.

*Slugs and Snails* do enormous damage, much of it unseen below soil level. Slugs feed all the year, snails hibernate in rubbish, behind rocks, etc.

Use a bait containing Metaldehyde.

*Thrips* are small black "midges" which do little damage out of doors, but often spoil the look of plants by scraping the surface tissue.

Spray with malathion.

*Virus diseases* are carried in the sap and spread by sucking insects or even the gardener's hands and tools. Attacked plants look unhappy or stunted, often with an unusual "spiky" appearance or a rolling, crinkling or mottling of the leaves.

No cure. Burn badly infected plants, keep control of aphids and other sucking insects, buy only healthy plants from reliable sources.

*Weevils* Small beetles with snout-like heads; feed on leaves while their legless grubs feed on roots.

Trap in crumpled pieces of sacking or corrugated paper.

*Wireworms* are shiny yellowish-brown grubs seen particularly when old turf is broken up. Take five years to mature and reach $\frac{3}{4}$ in. in length; feed on plant roots or cause seedlings to wilt and die.

Trap in pieces of potato or carrot, dust with BHC.

*Wood lice* Keep everything tidy; dust with BHC.

## OTHER DISEASES

In addition to the general diseases given above, there are a number which are confined to certain groups of plants only. The more important are:

*Apple blossom weevil* grubs feed on the flower, the dead petals forming a brown cap.

Use proprietary spray or dust, just before the flower-buds open.

*Apple and Pear scab* causes dark patches on young leaves, quickly becoming brownish-black. Later, fruits show black spots and cracks.

Spray with lime-sulphur or proprietary captan spray.

*Apple suckers* are small, flat, yellowish to green sticky insects found in young leaves and blossoms. Buds die or fail to set fruit.

Spray with malathion.

*Big bud of currants* Minute mites live in the buds which swell and fail to open and fruit.

Pick off and burn infected buds or spray with lime-sulphur (1% solution) when leaves are the size of a two-shilling piece and before flowers open.

*Black spot of roses* causes black spots or blotches on the leaves which fall and may end in complete defoliation.

Remove and burn infected leaves, use proprietary captan or thiram spray.

*Brown rot* causes many kinds of fruit to rot and drop off.
Collect and burn infected fruit.

*Cabbage caterpillars* occur on all brassicas and must be controlled while young before they enter the developing hearts, by spraying with derris.

*Cabbage root fly* attacks all brassicas, the grubs eating the roots, causing wilting or a blue, stunted appearance.

Dust around plants with calomel or BHC and, as a preventive, dust when planting.

*Cabbage white fly* A small fly usually doing little harm unless it gets into the hearts.

Pick off and burn any lower leaves having eggs or larvae on undersides; burn old stumps from an infected crop; spray with malathion.

*Canker* Several fungi cause a dry decay of branches of many trees, generally in the form of a depressed or ragged area; whole shoots may die back.

Cut out and burn infected parts; destroy badly attacked trees; always prune carefully and cover cuts and wounds with grafting wax.

*Carrot fly* causes the foilage to wilt and turn reddish. Roots are attacked by small colourless maggots.

Sow thinly to avoid singling; in bad areas defer sowing till June; spray with BHC fortnightly.

*Club root,* common on brassicas and some flowers, causes rough swellings on the roots. Plants look blue and stunted.

Lime regularly; avoid growing on infected soil or dip plants in a paste of moistened calomel dust before planting.

*Codling moth* (principally on apples) eats out the centre of the fruit in late summer.

After bad attacks, use proprietary spray the following year fourteen days after petal-fall.

*Fire blight* occurs on certain shrubs and trees, the pear Laxton's Superb being particularly susceptible. Leaves wilt and turn brown but hang on the tree as though damaged by fire. The disease must be notified to the Ministry of Agriculture who will advise on control.

*Moths* of many kinds cause harm by their caterpillars eating and sometimes stripping the foilage of trees and shrubs. Some form tents or webs as protection.

Spray with malathion; break up tents.

*Narcissus fly* The grubs live inside the bulb, which gives only a weak or distorted growth.

Avoid planting soft bulbs; in bad attacks, dust with BHC every fourteen days during May or June.

*Onion fly* Small, whitish maggots burrow into the bulbs; the leaves and stems turn yellow.

Burn infected plants; dust with calomel.

*Onion smut* causes dark greyish stripes on the leaves, which wilt.

Burn infected plants and avoid growing on the same ground.

*Pea moth* caterpillars eat the peas in the pod.

Hoe regularly to destroy pupae in the soil.

*Peach leaf curl* causes swollen, curled or blistered leaves.

Use copper-lime proprietary spray when buds are about to break.

*Potato blight* causes patches on the leaves, brown to black on top, greyish underneath. Later the tubers may be infected, showing the well-known brownish colour under the skin.

Spray with proprietary copper-lime spray as soon as disease appears and every fortnight as necessary.

*Potato scab* causes rough, dry, scabby patches on the skin.

Improve soil by adding farmyard manure or compost. Do not dress with lime.

*Potato wart disease* causes crinkled warts at the base of the stems and on the tubers of susceptible varieties.

Grow immune varieties only.

*Raspberry beetle* causes "maggoty" fruits.

Spray or dust with derris ten days after flowering and again twelve–fourteen days later.

*Reversion of Black currants* causes small, narrow leaves and no crop.

Grub-up and burn and replace with healthy stock.

*Silver leaf* on certain fruit and ornamental trees is caused by a fungus separating the top and bottom surfaces of the leaf, which appears silvery.

Remove all dead wood by early summer every year, cover cuts and wounds with grafting wax.

*Tulip fire* causes streaks on the leaves, and the tips to become brown and scorched.

Lift bulbs every year and burn unsound ones. Avoid planting in the same soil for four or five years.

*Woolly aphis,* a purple-coloured aphid protected by a white fluff, is most common on apples.

Spray with malathion.

# Index

94